SA   RY

D0099107

2010

FOOD
HEROES

16 Culinary Artisans

PRESERVING TRADITION

FOOD HEROES

16 Culinary Artisans

PRESERVING TRADITION

GEORGIA PELLEGRINI

Stewart, Tabori & Chang ✳ New York

For Anne "Aunty" Lepori,
whose pastina set the tempo to my life

Published in 2010 by Stewart, Tabori & Chang
An imprint of ABRAMS

Text copyright © 2010 Georgia Pellegrini
Photographs copyright © 2010 Georgia Pellegrini

All rights reserved. No portion of this book may be reproduced, stored in a retrieval system, or transmitted in any form or by any means, mechanical, electronic, photo-copying, recording, or otherwise, without written permission from the publisher.

Library of Congress Cataloging-in-Publication Data

Pellegrini, Georgia.
  Food heroes : sixteen culinary artisans preserving tradition / Georgia Pellegrini.
    p. cm.
  Includes bibliographical references and index.
  ISBN 978-1-58479-854-5 (alk. paper)
  1. Gastronomy. 2. Cookery. 3. Food crops. 4. Natural foods. I. Title.
  TX631.P45 2010
  641.013—dc22

                        2010003754

Editor: Dervla Kelly
Designer: Anna Christian
Production Manager: Tina Cameron

The text of this book was composed in Jenson.

Printed and bound in the United States of America
10 9 8 7 6 5 4 3 2 1

Stewart, Tabori & Chang books are available at special discounts when purchased in quantity for premiums and promotions as well as fundraising or educational use. Special editions can also be created to specification. For details, contact specialsales@abramsbooks.com or the address below.

THE ART OF BOOKS SINCE 1949
115 West 18th Street
New York, NY 10011
www.abramsbooks.com

CONTENTS

INTRODUCTION

I can still picture her standing in her gardens, permanently hunched over, with shovel and trowel, her white hair puffing out from below the brim of her baseball hat, her floral skirt falling just above her muddy oversized sneakers. My father's aunt, Ann Gray, was my first food hero. When I was growing up, Aunt Gray and I would take long walks through the fields where she and I were both raised, in Sparkill, a tiny hamlet in New York's Hudson Valley, and she would point out every tree and shrub that her father, my great-grandfather, had planted. When she died the metallic labels she used to identify her plants still twinkled in the sun as a reminder of her determination to preserve old varieties.

Aunt Gray was famous for her rustic cornbread, as well as for her homemade ice cream, which she prepared with the bare minimum of sugar in order to let the other flavors come through. She probably would have eliminated sugar from her recipes altogether if she could have gotten away with it, such was her disdain for added sweetener. Some people may have found her cooking a bit too austere, but our family grew to appreciate her Puritanical approach; thanks to her, I learned to make my jellies and tarts taste even better with less sugar.

Aunt Gray never had children, but nonetheless seems to have exerted her influence on my father as he grew up. Though born in the most urban of environments, he was brought back to "the country" by the age of six and soon became a devout exurbanite. He, too, came to learn the name of every plant on our land and added labels of his own. He planted quince trees and greengage plums, built beehives and filled them with Russian and Italian honeybees, and constructed chicken coops teeming with Rhode Island Reds. As a teenager, I'd sit on a boulder by the creek with my dad, push a fat worm onto a hook, and fish for trout, which we fried up in the skillet for breakfast. I snipped wild chives from the bottom of the back stairs for omelets and salads. I became the self-proclaimed wild raspberry queen, battling the birds every late July so I would have enough fruit to make jam.

After moving to New England for college, the path of least resistance lured me back to New York and into the world of finance. But as

I sat blurry-eyed from scrutinizing Excel spreadsheets, and watched the cafeteria dinner cart roll by night after night, my yearning for the kitchen consumed me. And so I traded Wall Street for culinary school, diving into *tournage, fond,* consommé, *pâte brisée* and *sucrée, crème patisserie,* and *pâte à choux.* There I made petite éclair swans filled with pastry cream, pear tarts with frangipane, braised shanks, and glazed vegetables carved into equally sized ovals. It was endless and exhausting and satisfying.

I met my next inspiration, Kristian, on my first day as a line cook at Blue Hill at Stone Barns in the Hudson Valley. He was the fish cook, and when he slid out of the cold room balancing trays of butterflied trout on his palm, everyone, including me, turned to look. Tall and thin, he wore tight black pants and white slip-on clogs, and his brown hair was slicked back into a ponytail. When he spoke, his voice was so soft I could barely understand him—it was like another language: half whisper, half French.

Kristian taught me something significant every day. He stood by my side, our cheeks inches apart, and I watched him turn chives into delicate rings as thin as strands of hair. He showed me how to bring them to my lips and feel the texture on my tongue. "This is how chives should feel when they are sliced properly," he would say. Like texture on the tip of the tongue.

For me, life at Stone Barns was a return to the natural order of things, and my work there catapulted me back to my childhood. On Thursdays, Kristian and I collected eggs before going into the kitchen. We jumped over the electric fence and gathered as many eggs as we could before the chickens began pecking at our toes. When the work was brutal, when our bodies were stiff from lifting heavy crates and our ears rang from the frenetic yelling of the kitchen bosses, we picked flowers for the stations in the kitchen. Some nights, just around midnight, we went into the attic and sorted through boxes of tomatoes, separating the perfect ones from those acceptable for staff meal, and those to be turned into tomato water. He taught me the names of heirloom tomatoes—Green Zebra, Garden Peach, Banana Legs—and the different feeling each one has against the skin. The earthy smell of rotten tomatoes was something I grew to love.

Marion the forager, who often came to visit the kitchen with her latest discoveries, became another hero. She brought oyster mushrooms, some of which were a beautiful green—a sign that the mushroom season was coming to an end. She invited me along on some of her hunts, where she'd spend an evening lurking in the shadows of her neighbors' yards, cutting mushrooms off their trees with her knife. "Mushrooms bring out the gypsy in me," she would say with a smile.

At Stone Barns, I dreamt about butternut squash consommé, and weeding Savoy spinach in the greenhouse became my therapy. I learned the particularly cleansing feeling of eating a tart green apple at 2 A.M. at the end of a fifteen-hour shift. I handled five hundred animal parts in a day—breasts, thighs, chicken oysters, lamb necks, cured pork bellies, and cured beef bellies—and rubbed up against hanging pig carcasses while struggling to load trays full of meat into walk-in refrigerators. The deep, musty smell of Marsala lingering with cooking morels signaled the change of the season. As did the slaughter of the turkeys. They were stunning creatures, brown with feathers fanned out, their high-pitched gobbles echoing in the woods by the creek.

The first time I killed a turkey, the smell of wet feathers lingered for weeks. For a while I couldn't tell if it was in my head or still on my hands. Wet feathers smell like a wet dog—mildly sweet and warm, but not very pleasant. We had killed five Broad Breasted Whites in the sheep meadow in a matter of minutes. I stood paralyzed as the cooks chased them down. Each time one was caught I hoped it would escape, but the slaughter was less dramatic than I expected. One person pinned the bird down while another cut the windpipe. The birds seemed peaceful even as they beat their wings and gasped for air. We held them down until their bodies went limp. All of the surviving turkeys gathered at the fence to watch, and I remember wanting to cover their collective eyes. We dunked the dead bodies in boiling water and plucked them. White feathers filled the air and floated in the sunlight. Then the omnivore in me kicked in and I thrust my hands deep into a bird's cavity. It was still warm. I slid my hands up the inside of the breastbone and felt the windpipe and heart and gizzard and intestines, and pulled them out in one handful. I severed its feet and head and removed the yellow gland at its tail. I sliced open the gizzard and pulled out the sack of grain it had eaten that morning, the grain still whole.

Working with ingredients in their purest state sealed my resolve to work in places that supported local growers and valued authentic flavors. It also motivated me to continue to seek out others who felt the same craving for natural flavors that I did, and who were willing to fight to ensure that real food was readily available as an answer to processed foods.

After a year at Stone Barns, I moved back to Manhattan, where I discovered that food heroes are not just quietly foraging in the woods of the countryside—they are everywhere, even in one of the densest cities on earth. Among the many places in the city devoted to local ingredients is Gramercy Tavern, the mother ship of Manhattan restaurants, where lines formed an hour before the doors opened and reservations were full within the first five minutes of the phone lines opening. It was here that I found my next job. I spent my days whisking cold butter into a warm sauce until it shined and emulsified, and served eighty people per hour in temperatures so hot my eyelashes curled; I earned scars on my arms from burns and often smelled like a campfire by day's end. It was here that I met oyster enthusiast Jon Rowley, who recruited me to shuck oysters for him and gleefully told me about the virtues of the briny Olympia oyster. And it was here that I cooked for avid regulars like Mr. Munyan, a man who had been eating quail on a bed of plain frisée with a side of limas in the same seat at the same table every Sunday at 12 P.M. sharp for ten years—until the fateful Sunday when I decided to make him green beans instead. After that, he ignored most of his other food and devoured green beans every Sunday.

I often watched Mr. Munyan eat by the big window while I fed white oak into the wood-burning stove. He was well into his eighties, a thin silver mop on his head, his cane propped against the side of his chair. He wore a suit to dine alone and always called ahead, as if it were his first time. "May I join you for lunch today?" he'd ask politely. He ordered a $500 bottle of Bordeaux on most days and never finished it. Some of the best wine I tasted was the leftover bottle the sommelier left in the kitchen for me to try. Mr. Munyan taught me the value in sitting down for a proper meal, and our Sunday exchange of beans for Bordeaux was a ritual I looked forward to.

Soon, though, not even perfect little oysters, nor sips from a $500 bottle of wine, could keep me in a New York kitchen any longer, and so I did what others before me have done: I traveled to France, where I got a job at La Chassagnette, a destination restaurant in Provence with its own organic gardens. The pace of rural life in the south of France was an exercise in extreme patience for someone who had the current of New York City coursing through her veins. I lived in a run-down house crowded with frogs and cobwebs set back into a deep field along the Rhône River. I slept under a tablecloth I took from the restaurant and woke to the sulfur smell of the marsh every morning, a particular Camargue charm that I never did get used to. My head spun with French words, the French language a thousand little dots in my head, which connected at random moments, while rolling out pasta dough or pulling heads off sardines. The executive chef wore a blue denim apron and sneakers with leopard fur, which meant I rarely heard him coming.

The kitchen at La Chassagnette was a mosh pit of dysfunction. Knives waved in the air in dramatic protest; people called each other's names from unreasonable distances. I mastered the art of skinning a fish without a knife—and then learned how to do it in the dark when the power went out. Pretty soon I could strip a fish cavity clean in the time it took someone to say, "*La lumière, la lumière, je m'en charge!*" There were also plenty of moments like the time I peeled the skin off fifty grapes and deseeded them with a paper clip, only to watch the chef pop them in his mouth like candy a few minutes later.

My respite was hiding in the garden house with the old gardener Emmanuel and his three-legged cat. He taught me about unusual herbs and all their attributes and the potency of greens grown in dry heat and little rain. He taught me to stop and smell the rosemary and murmured "*Une américaine avec le courage,*" as he watched me discover my love for driving heavy farm equipment.

On days when I approached the edges of insanity in the kitchen, I escaped with Eric, the food buyer for the restaurant, to the farmers' market, where I observed the forceful debates among locals on the merits of various foods and the best ways to prepare them. In France there was always time to stop and discuss these important matters. Wherever they might be going or when they might be expected to arrive, it could wait.

Food came first. I learned my French numbers working the farmers' market, and watched as one old lady pressed her thumbs firmly into a *cebette* (a French vegetable in the leek family), while another man walked by loudly singing the name of each vegetable as he inspected them.

I spent my last weeks in France visiting Francis, our fig supplier, at Les Figuières, where we ate the last figs of the season off his trees and reminisced. I dined with a bottle of rosé while I waited for the chicken supplier to finish killing her chickens. (Eric had taught me never to arrive early when picking up your ingredients since they may still be alive.) I spent afternoons rolling through the hills of Les Baux-de-Provence with Jean-Benoît, the owner of an olive oil farm, watching his olive harvest. He poured the first bottle of the year's olive oil and gave it to me to remember him by. As if I could ever forget.

———

Today, artisanal methods are in retreat and, in many cases, live mostly in the memory and imagination of older generations. Once, in local villages and towns from the American Southwest to Eastern Europe were found Spanish frittatas, Tennessee "hot" chicken, Arkansas tamales, bowls of Alsatian sauerkraut, simmered Modena *cotechino* sausage, and piles of Krakow dumplings—dishes created and brought to the table from the surrounding countryside and imbued with local character. It is the kind of food that stimulates a core satisfaction rarely found even in the most acclaimed restaurants of our time. It will vary in taste and appearance with the season and the soil and from one town to the next. Yet it is food that is always tempered by family tradition and the habits of the generations who pass it down; food that gains meaning from our knowledge of its origins, where it came from, who prepared it and how. When this tie to tradition is undone, food is much less satisfying.

The chain of supply is broken when farmers' markets are overrun with middlemen instead of farmers, or when laws require a woman with only three dozen eggs to sell to keep careful records. It is a noble person who still takes the time to locate a supply of old-fashioned ingredients today. Paychecks go first to cell phones and glossy entertainment. Where people once gathered their water from a well and found their pleasure at the table, today they seek satisfaction in the drive-through. In response, chefs today seduce patrons with novelty and food pyrotechnics; little towers of nothing in the center of oversized plates, while customers are increasingly distracted by what is currently stamped "healthy." Artisanal beer is abandoned for a lower-calorie version. Fat is avoided like the plague. And as a result, good food has lost its luster.

America's food culture is in the midst of a pendulum swing. The big-label brands that once filled our kitchen cupboards have been replaced in many homes by mass-market organics. We are more conscious now of where our food originates. But as the steady current of neatly pack-aged "whole foods" continues and feel-good marketing prevails, we are left missing the point. The counterintuitive USDA standards for "organically grown" have become so far removed from what organic once meant that the word has lost its meaning. And as "agri-tourism" booms, and people purposefully meander to the country with their kids on the weekends, "local" and "sustainable" are starting to sound a tad precious, even condescending.

But as with most things, there is a silver lining. The disconnect between the accelerating pace of life and our natural human roots is making our hunger for tradition and a simpler life ever greater. When we garden rather than buy from the grocery store, when we intention-ally buy from people who have chosen a rough-hewn life in order to produce something truly good, we are saying, whether we realize it or not, that we are craving something. There is a natural human instinct to be in touch with our roots, to use our hands, to create things. And regardless of the ever-widening gap between modern life and the natu-ral world, it is nearly impossible to eliminate that instinct.

Trying economic times are the great equalizer. As many are forced to look for meaning outside the confines of corporate life, they seek to reclaim some of that lost connection, a life more connected to nature, a way to live more closely to the land. They are hunting for what is real and lasting versus what is fake and manufactured. As more diversified small farms pop up with younger operators, as city-dwellers endeavor to keep honeybees on their high-rise rooftops, they are finding ways, large and small, to step ever so slightly off the grid. I predict that this is only the beginning.

In this book, I track down the origins of ancient foods that have captured my heart and imagination—and my palate. I seek simple food, ingredients that are anchored to the seasons and a specific place; the kind of food once served in simple restaurants and in homes by housewives, by grandmothers, by families for generations, and today by people—culinary artisans—choosing to do the hard work required to live off the best their hands can produce.

What follows are stories of ordinary people doing extraordinary things with food while living and thriving outside a corporate urban environment. With family cooking on the wane and tradition increasingly under attack, the highest and best practices and ingredients of traditional cooking are being preserved by these artisans. This is my gastronomical journey to find the last vestiges of culinary tradition, and the people and places behind this food. Whether they are going up against the government in order to preserve the traditional method of dry-cured sausages, or going up against Mother Nature to keep disappearing potato varieties in national collections, these are people who are taking extraordinary measures to preserve good taste. When these values die, it is like setting a library on fire. Welcome to the world of sausage makers, mushroom hunters, cheese makers, and chance takers: the people who make food a craft and a life's meaning—the food heroes of our time.

DAVID LANGFORD

The Potato Protector

CHAPTER ONE

The Potato Breeder

I t begins at the gates of a carriage house in Sligo, Ireland, where the air smells like roasting cumin. It takes place in the gardens of Lissadell House, inside four ancient brick walls that hold the largest tuber collection in the world. Up a wooded dirt road I go, the Irish Sea crashing against the shoreline at my back. And there David Langford awaits, his hands clasped neatly behind him, a silver goatee flattering his satisfied smile.

The limestone walls are gray and tired; they hint at a former comeliness tarnished by time. This was once a distinguished horticultural estate, and now Lissadell is climbing back to its place in history. On the way, Lissadell found Langford, a man who, like his potatoes, is able to thrive wherever he is deposited.

He has spent his life nowhere and everywhere, from the Arctic to the Antarctic, and all around the "Med." Though born an Irishman, he spent his life with his father, ensconced in the British military; he moved thirty-eight times as a child and nineteen times as an adult. Along the way he found himself looking at spuds, very strange potatoes, and was fascinated by them.

Many years later, he is finally stationary. He lives in a two-hundred-year-old house with its original flagstone floors, bog oak beams, and grand fireplace. And he spends his days at Lissadell, tending to 180 varieties of rare potatoes. The spuds now come to him; strangers send them from around the world—often varieties lost in one culture are found in another. Each new tuber that arrives in his mailbox is a time capsule, a reflection of someone's personal history. Here he plants them for everyone, one of only three men left in the world on a mission to preserve dying potato varieties and put them back into national collections. Norway, Holland, Russia . . . they arrive, and he dutifully tucks them into the garden, six inches deep under a blanket of soil.

He stands effervescent over a table full of potatoes nestled in wicker baskets in shades of pink, purple, gray, and brown, and exclaims, "I'm a great lover of traditional everything. My whole family loved old things. My mother's people were carpenters, and made furniture. We weren't a rich family, but we always had fine things about us that had been made in workshops." He reaches down and turns a potato tenderly in his thick palm. "Seventeen seventy," he says. "See how many eyes?" The potato looks like a tired old man, full of little wobbly bits, but weathered in a noble kind of way. "I'm a great believer in traditional cookery. I cook right back to the seventeen hundreds." His singularly perfect meal is roasted potatoes mixed with apples, onions, and one sage leaf, with an accompaniment of roast pork.

It has been a wet summer in Sligo. The temperate, misty climate stirs the silhouette of W. B. Yeats, a Sligo boy, who played cricket matches on this verdant grass, kicked around the oyster beds behind the shore walls, and evoked its beauty and genius in his poetry. A friend of the heir to Lissadell, Eva Gore-Booth, he slept here from time to time, often relegated to the carriage house where guests stayed when the main house was full. Victorian greenhouses still perch a few steps away on the outskirts of the two-and-a-half-acre kitchen garden, home to cherry tomatoes and baby greens with precious names like Ruby Streaks and Golden Frills. Then, as now, this is one of the foremost potato-growing places in the world. When the Great Hunger arrived in the nineteenth century, famine relief was provided to thousands inside this place. From here "peace comes dropping slow," Yeats said. "I hear lake water lapping with low sounds by the shore, I hear it in the deep heart's core."

Through the wooden gates beyond its weathered walls, the kitchen garden is like the secret garden, a mossy, magic plot where twenty-nine varieties of lettuce mingle with nine types of basil, and a few steps away those 180 potato varieties are planted chronologically by date, two tubers every three feet.

We walk the trimly carved paths: I, Langford, and Dermot Cary, the head gardener. They are an odd pair: David short and stocky with a tidy silver beard and well-worn fishing vest, Dermot tall and thin with wispy locks. They banter in a thick Irish brogue about types of potatoes, flavors, facts, likes, and dislikes. David calls Dermot "a man of the soil."

David kneels to inspect his potatoes, then talks about them expressively as if they are his girlfriends. "Arran Victory are a gorgeous spud. They're a wonderful baked potato. They're a purple, purple skin with a lovely white flesh . . . floury . . . they make lovely everything. And they make the most wonderful roasters when you roll them in goose fat." He bubbles over with knowledge and optimism, becoming dreamy. "And the Highland Burgundy Red, it's a lovely pink. Beautiful pink chips and pink mash. . . ." He trails off wistfully, as if contemplating a lover.

Dermot, more staid, makes his rounds, the pebbles crunching like a good lettuce under his feet. For him, each potato carries significant history, and also challenges. These varieties are rarely seen in stores because heirlooms aren't as efficient to grow commercially. "You have factors like yield, disease resistance, taste, shelf life. Commercial growers have to compromise to grow on a large scale. I'm lucky because I can take them from the ground and put them right into our store."

David adds, "People ask me, 'why can't I get these varieties in the market?' And the answer is because commercial growers don't want to put in the effort to grow them! It's a shame. We are depriving people of great taste!"

He tries his best to disseminate heirloom potatoes, encouraging and helping others to grow them. He was giving one of his talks recently and a man about eighty years old came up to him and told him he'd been trying to find a potato from his childhood called Hadrian's Heel and asked him if he'd come across it. David had never heard of it. A few weeks later someone sent him three tiny spuds, each the size of a thumbnail. They were labeled "Hadrian's Heel." "I sent them to him, and his wife tells me that he carries the potato spuds around with him all day in a bucket to keep them in the sun. To me it's so worthwhile. That's why I'm so passionate about it."

David's potatoes are a reflection of personal history, each one the essence of a particular time and place. Very few people in the Western world still eat real potatoes, he says plaintively. Microwavable mashed potatoes are among the most popular potato products in the United Kingdom; one can squeeze them out of a tube like lumpy toothpaste.

"In a survey of schoolchildren in Yorkshire, sixty percent thought potatoes came from trees. Over ninety percent couldn't identify a leek. Most had never seen cabbages and didn't know what chard was. Now, that is appalling!" he says, animated. "You know, I'm old, I'm getting past it. The reality is when my generation goes, a lot of the new generation won't have a clue what to do with this stuff. If they can't buy it and microwave it, they're going to starve."

As part of his mission he teaches people how to grow potatoes in a garbage bag. Three spuds in a bag yields up to twenty pounds of potatoes. "Look," he says to his cadre of potato apostles, "get three potatoes that are a different variety than you're used to, and put them in a bag, and at the end of the year, try them, and if you like them, grow a row!" And the apostles dutifully return to him, delighted. "Try that. Fantastic," they say. Potatoes will grow at elevations from zero to fifteen hundred feet, and are flexible in varying climates. But they don't like to be grown in the same place twice, which is why David grows his in forty-liter pots that he puts right into the ground. It keeps the varieties well separated. And because they are so old and rare, he adds clean compost every year to reduce the chance of disease.

Disease has plagued the potato throughout history, which is why the potato has morphed into so many varieties, every potato the descendent of a single primordial spud. As they succumb to blight they change and reform themselves into newer versions. So while old potato varieties provide a historical timeline, the true glory of the potato is that it is naturally evolving. The older the variety, the more dimples or "eyes" it has, and as we crossbreed, the eyes disappear, leaving an array of shiny, smooth-skinned spuds.

We descend now into the centuries-old root cellar where wooden crates of potatoes live with exquisite little pears. David calls himself a "potato nut," and Dermot a "rotten devil," as they banter and sift through, in search of a particular tuber. "Arran Victory," they say in collective swoon. "Purple skin . . . with very light flesh. Those explode to absolute flower," David sighs. Then comes the Easter-egg pink Sarpo Mira. "I wouldn't torture my enemy with them! That's horrible, it's vile!" Then the low-carb Vivaldi. "That's called the slimmer's potato because it has one third the carbohydrates of the others, but a potato is not fattening unless you stick a lot of butter in it." Then the Pink Fir Apple: "Those are good salad potatoes because the flesh doesn't crumble." And then the one that makes his skin crawl, the Bambino. "If I have a show I have a tag that says, 'This is the worst potato I've ever tasted.' If you boiled it today for an hour, steamed it tomorrow for two hours, roasted it for a week, you wouldn't be able to eat it. It's vile! Absolutely, disgustingly vile. If you mashed it, oh my God, you could build walls with the results!"

The range of potato textures varies from "waxy" to "floury." Salad potatoes like the Pink Fir Apple are waxy, and stay together when cooked. They have a nutty flavor and are the style most favored in Britain. The Irish prefer a floury potato, which can disintegrate and absorb a lot of butter. If not cooked properly these potatoes have a floury taste. David's personal favorite is the floury Golden Wonder, a potato from 1916. "It is amazing how different countries have different preferences," he says. "England likes a wet waxy type potato like King Edward and Maris Piper, whereas Ireland likes the floury types like Rooster, Record, and Kerr's Pink. The French prefer waxy types, the Scots floury types and so on. Each type has its merits for different types of cooking, the wetter waxy type are good for chips. The Maris Piper is the one that most chip shops use in Britain and Ireland, whereas floury potatoes are perfect for mash and roasting." The most popular to come out of Lissadell today is the tan, smooth-skinned Orla. But it is hard to find these lovely things, because no one wants to grow them. It is easier to grow a few standard varieties and sell them en masse. Worse still, the average nonorganic potato is sprayed with trichloro dichlorophenyl ethane eighteen times in the field and nine times in the store to fix small cuts and fungus, which means the perfect-looking potato is sprayed twenty-seven times before it gets to the plate.

In November 2008, David flew to Rome to talk to the United Nations about spuds, after the United Nations declared 2008 the International Year of the Potato. David joined the International Potato Committee in order to get more third-world countries to grow more potatoes in place of rice, maize, and barley. Throw a potato into a fire and you have a meal—no milling or processing required. With more nutrition in potatoes per acre, it is one solution to food shortages. Convincing people to incorporate the potato into their diet is the challenge, since it is not inextricably linked to the cultures and palates of some countries. But the potato's popularity is rising in third-world countries while declining in wealthy ones. Fast-food chains, trans–fat–laden potato chips, and frozen French fries make it increasingly difficult to convince children in developed countries to eat potatoes that have not been heavily processed. And it means the beauty and variety of full-flavored heirlooms is rapidly disappearing.

Inside the carriage house we sit sipping tea and eating warm ginger cake, a bucket of beautiful spuds next to me. "Is there anything outside the spud world?" David says buoyantly, peering over the rim of his spectacles.

"I was giving one of my talks recently and afterwards a one-hundred-year-old man came up to me. He had his son with him, who had his son with him, who had his son with him. The oldest son asked me, 'Can the old man hold the potatoes?' I said of course. He told me about the varieties of potatoes that his father and grandfather used to have. At the end I asked, 'Would the old man like to pick ten varieties to take home with him?' And he did. A few months later the potatoes prompted a family reunion and all the brothers and uncles came together from around the world. They called me from the party and said they were all sitting around the table in tears reflecting on two hundred years of their family's history with the potato. It dated back before the famine. Now that's worth it, isn't it?"

The room smells of cleanliness; the stone floors, walls, shelves, and all the dark wood beams emit a cool air. David sips his tea and sighs. "Some people have lost their roots. They no longer even think about doing things the traditional way because they are so far removed from it." In his small village, he has become the friendly tradition police, challenging his neighbors and friends to traditional cooking competitions, to cake baking rather than cake buying. "Instead of buying biscuits and cakes, we've found all these lovely recipes. It's been a revelation; some of these ladies are superb bakers. And they've not baked some of these dishes for twenty or thirty years. Their mothers taught them to bake, their grannies taught them to bake, and they just packed it up because the money was available. But now with the economic downturn, I think a lot more people will go back to having to bake, having to make their own cooked stews, and what have you, with the cheaper cuts of meat, and all the rest of it. I think a lot of people are frightened to even think about doing it because the skills are not there anymore. But I say, why not try it?"

David's life has been about trying it, about finding the fountainhead. And helping others to as well. "Whenever the feeling is weightiest, you are at your best," Yeats once told the Lissadell heiress inside these walls. And for David Langford the feeling of this weight, his purpose, is profound.

✍ A RECIPE FOR BOXTY

Adapted from the dozens of papers that David has collected.

Boxty is a potato-pancake dish without discernible origins. Although the name is Irish, the dish is not. When David requested boxty recipes from communities in Northern Ireland he was flooded with mail, and the recipes were all different. Old women had learned them from their ancestors mostly through word of mouth. The same ancient recipes can be found in India, Russia, Scotland, England, and right through Europe. Boxty is everywhere, but no one knows where it came from.

This recipe is a basic version. It can be used as a base and then enhanced to your liking with savory or sweet bits: For savory boxty, add grated onion, herbs, cheese, and peppers, a hint of cayenne or a handful of chopped cooked ham. For sweet ones, add grated apple, raisins that have been soaking in a bath of rum, honey, or spices.

> 3 medium potatoes
> 2 cups milk
> 1 cup all-purpose flour
> 1 teaspoon salt, plus more for sprinkling
> ½ teaspoon baking powder
> Butter
> Black pepper

1. Peel and grate the potatoes, either by hand or in a food processor.
2. In a bowl, combine the potatoes with the milk, flour, salt, and baking powder, and mix well.
3. Drop tablespoons of the mixture into a hot buttered skillet, and pat them so they are about ½ inch thick. Cook over medium-low heat, turning until golden on both sides, adding butter as needed along the way.
4. Transfer the boxty to a paper towel and sprinkle with salt and pepper to keep them crisp.

MAKES 12 TO 14 MEDIUM PANCAKES

✺ POTATO GNOCCHI

These gnocchi, when left raw, will freeze well on a flat baking sheet or tray, for another day. As a variation, you can add 1 teaspoon of grated grapefruit, orange, or lime zest, or for an earthy flavor add 1 teaspoon freshly grated nutmeg. I sometimes brown the gnocchi in a pan with oil or butter before adding a sauce, which gives them a better flavor and texture.

> *4 medium potatoes*
> *1 teaspoon salt*
> *1 cup all-purpose flour, plus more if not using Wondra for dusting*
> *3 large egg yolks*
> *Wondra flour (optional)*

1. Preheat the oven to 400°F.
2. Bake the potatoes for about 1 hour, until cooked through.
3. Peel the potatoes and pass them through a food mill or ricer. Add 1 teaspoon salt and the 1 cup all-purpose flour and combine until just mixed together, then stir in the egg yolks.
4. On a floured work surface, roll the dough gently with your palms into long, thin ropes, then cut the ropes into 1-inch pieces. Dust with Wondra or all-purpose flour.
5. Press one side of each gnocchi against the teeth of a clean hair comb or fork to give them their distinctive ridges.
6. Bring a large pot of well-salted water to a low simmer and add 10 gnocchi at a time; cook for about 30 seconds, until they float to the surface, then remove with a slotted spoon. Serve with a sauce.

MAKES 6 SERVINGS

ALLAN BENTON

The Hog Smoker

CHAPTER TWO

Madisonville, Tennessee

Smoking Hog

I n the fog of the Smoky Mountains, the pace of life shifts. The road from Nashville to Madisonville is a walkway to an alternate world where the hillsides are speckled with languid cows, and road signs loom through gray mist with hopeful messages—"Life Is Good," "Seriously Good Chicken," and "Jesus Saves." Every so often a colossal crucifix interrupts the skyline as a reminder that you are in God's country now. Next to a trailer, a horse stands motionless, and soon more signs appear inviting you to Frontier Firearms and the Budget Inn. This repeats and repeats until high above a country highway appears a sign: "Benton's Smoky Country Hams."

Two wrapped hams dangle by a string from the porch roof of a cinderblock store. A lanky man looks down over the railing, balancing a cigarette in the corner of his mouth.

"How you makin' it today?" he asks.

"I'm great. How are you?" I reply.

"Pretty good, pretty good."

"I'm here to see Allan Benton."

He grins. "Go on in and take a number."

Inside the store lobby, the rotary phone rings at a fever pitch, and the encompassing smell of hog fat and hickory smoke flare up my nose. Locals in blue jeans and plaid shirts loiter patiently on all sides of the room. They are here for ham, and seem to possess an endless willingness to wait. Some sit on benches gazing into the distance, toothpicks clenched between their teeth. One orders a sandwich with smoked ham and American cheese from a glass cooler. Another is happy just standing there, allowing the ambient smells of smoked meat to soak into his pores.

Standing behind a worn wooden counter next to a rack of cured pork parts, adorned in checkered flannel, is Allan Benton. "We're gonna get you taken care of," he says softly to a woman who drove three hours for a side of bacon. Then turning to me, he says, "The pleasure is all mine. We're just a hole-in-the-wall place, as you can see."

———

In 1973 Allan Benton realized he had made the wrong career choice as a college guidance counselor.

"I took one look at the salary schedule and I thought there was no way I could survive. I walked into the principal's office and I said, 'I can't do this, I can't work for this.' And he said, 'That's what it pays.' And I said, 'I know. I quit.' And he said, 'You're not serious.' And I said, 'I'm dead serious. I can't do this. I'm going to do something else.' And he said, 'What?' And I said, 'I don't know.' And I went home and told my dad that I quit and he said, 'Great, what are you gettin' into?' And I said, 'I don't know.' And he said, 'Son, that's not very prudent thinking.' I thought about law school, I thought about the insurance business, and then I heard that a man named Albert Hicks was selling this business."

So Allan Benton sat with Albert Hicks under a maple tree to see if he could take it over. Thirty-six years later Allan makes what some consider to be the best ham and bacon in the United States—an intoxicating combination of pork, salt, smoke, brown sugar, and time. He never intended to make a substantial living from it; he imagined it simply as a way of life with the single goal of producing exquisite hams and bacons. Now they are sought out by chefs and devoted customers around the country.

The Benton family spent their lives raising and killing hogs. Allan grew up in the depths of southern Appalachian poverty, where pork was the sustenance of the people. Pigs were easy to raise and easy to process, and you didn't have to have a lot of land to keep them. His grandparents turned their hogs loose in the woods of rural Virginia, the same way the Europeans do today to produce nutty-flavored pork like jamon Iberico, which sells for over $160 per pound. "My granddaddy would go out with a bucket of corn, and the hogs would come back from the woods," he says, gazing at a picture of the old farm on his wall.

His ancestors settled in the Virginia hill country, twenty-five miles from the nearest town. They built their house out of yellow poplar, and the original smokehouse still stands next door. "My grandmother, I remember her telling me when I was sixteen that that place would one day be mine. And she said I hope you'll never sell it, and I said, well, as long as I'm alive it'll never be sold. I remember telling her that, and I'll never sell it. I hope my son doesn't. I close my eyes and I can see my uncle with his horse and wagon. He would put on a suit coat and a clean white shirt, and I'd see him riding down to church every Sunday morning. It's a way of life that is quickly disappearing."

On the Benton farm in Virginia, Allan subsisted on his grandparents' homemade butter, homemade cottage cheese, and homegrown vegetables. They canned and preserved all that their land produced; nothing went to waste. "I have absolutely no reservations that it is the best way to eat," he says. "I think the ingredients you start with determine the quality of the product. It's like a cabinetmaker. To make a fine piece of cabinetry or furniture, you can't start with number-two pine. You have to start with select hardwood, the best stuff you can find. It's the same with meat."

Benton's original family recipe includes salt, brown sugar, and black and red pepper. He ages it for two months in a "salt room" at 38° to 43°F, then moves it to the equalization room for two to three months at 42° to 48°F, where the smell of ammonia pervades—an indication that the right type of mold is forming on the outside of the hams. At the end of the second stage, the hams have lost 16 to 18 percent of their fresh weight. He rolls wooden racks draped with these hams into his smokehouse and cold-smokes them at 90°F.

He produces thirteen to fourteen thousand hams and twenty thousand bacon bellies per year, compared to the one million hams per year produced by bigger country ham companies. He could produce more if he "quick-cured," but he thinks people would taste the difference.

When Allan bought the country ham business from Albert Hicks, he wrote to universities in the South trying to learn everything he could about dry-cured meat. He has spent the last thirty-six years trying to improve the appearance and flavor of his smoked hams, and seeking the best pork he can find. "I find myself being more and more resourceful. Anyplace that I find somebody's got a few hams that are grown organically from a heritage breed of hog that I think might be of extraordinary quality, I try to get them. I really believe that hillbillies here in the Southeast can produce just as good a product as our cousins over in Europe if we have a product as good to start with as they do. I don't think they have a dead lease on making grapes, prosciutto, or whatever over there. I think we can compete. I've always believed that we could. I'm not saying that we're doing it, but that's our goal. We're going to try every day to produce something that's world class and try to compete with our European cousins. There's no secret to what I do. It just takes a little bit of know-how and a lot of patience."

Outside, the smokehouse is small but packed, the smoke so thick you can't see past the doorway. Not too long ago it was still powered by an old fifty-dollar wood-burning stove, but now it is powered by a fireplace built into the brick wall. Allan kneels down and feeds hickory into the fire over the course of three to five days. The bacon cures for ten days and smokes for two. In total, his hams bearing the original family recipe will age for twelve months, and his regular country hams will age for eight to nine months. His prosciutto will average fifteen to sixteen months, and he is adamant that he will not sell it a day less than one year. He also does some custom curing from time to time.

Dangling on wooden racks in the main room, just above eye level, are hams with a surface like varnished mahogany—a product of hickory smoke and age. The oldest hams in the building are twenty-one months.

Some of them have a shinier appearance, which indicates the variety of hog and where it came from. Pigs put out to pasture feel more moist and greasy. "I can feel it with my eyes closed," he says, brushing the skin with his hand. "Modern hog farmers gravitate toward leaner and leaner pigs. People are afraid of fat. But it's a good fat that makes the difference."

In the wrapping room behind the counter, Allan and Arthur Atkins debone hams for their restaurant customers. Allan sticks his nose in the cavity and sniffs them repeatedly as he cuts the bone out. If it doesn't have the particular smell he is looking for, the warm smell of hog and the sweet smell of smoke, he discards it.

In the entrance, local farmers Eddie and Frank Griffith sit on a padded church pew that Eddie nailed to the wall himself years ago. Eddie wears very large overalls and Frank wears a baseball hat. In front of them are jars of chow-chow relish, Fischer's Red Hot Sausage, and bags of white corn grits. Blocks of American cheese are stacked inside a glass case, next to something called Charlie's souse (mild and hot), which they say is what people call headcheese up north.

The farmers grazing in the entrance speak at a barely audible pitch. They appear to be the most relaxed human beings I have ever met. They also have the most remarkable memories, their minds uncluttered. Everyone knows his ancestors' history in minute detail. They care about their roots and where they came from, and they tell me their stories as I strain to hear them above the drone of the meat slicer.

Eddie gives me a keen once-over before he begins to talk. He is in his seventies; his family raises animals and forages for ramps, the small wild leeks that grow in the Smoky Mountains. When I talk to him about ramps, he suddenly perks up. He is having difficulty getting up into the mountains these days, he says. But he thinks that maybe it's just laziness. "I cook them with some taters," he says. I say that I like to pickle them, and he is intrigued. He wants to know how big the ramps in the North get. He holds up his fat thumb to show me an example of how big they will get in the mountains of east Tennessee.

Arthur works the band saw in the background, slicing half-inch-thick ham slices for the meat-and-three restaurant a mile down the road. He wraps them in plastic wrap in groups of three, because that's the way they like it. He has been working here for five months longer than Allan has, when it was still owned by Albert Hicks. When Arthur is done slicing, he buys two sodas from the thirty-cent soda machine in the corner, hands me one, and joins the conversation.

Frank's cousin walks in to buy her summer supply of ham and bacon and sits herself right on the counter. She tells us that their cattle business isn't doing well this year, while Eddie continues his meanderings on food. He tells Frank that in the North they eat yellow cornbread. "Is that right?!" Frank is stunned. "I've never heard of it." In this part of the world, white corn bread is the standard. "Their gravy ain't the same either," Eddie continues, enjoying the audience. Their cousin chimes in to tell me how to make proper gravy while she waits for Arthur to collect her bacon. Red-eye gravy contains ham grease and a lot of coffee, the stronger the better. My lesson in "sawmill" gravy, made of milk and flour, is cut short when she and Eddie begin to bicker about the best way to make it. Eddie and Frank then tell me how to make "stack fruit cake," which contains dried apples in between the layers. "We dry them during the summer," Eddie tells me. "Allan eats a lot of cracklin' bread," he continues—bread studded with pieces of pork fat.

Allan comes over and describes to Frank what it is like to eat a lobster. Frank furrows his brow and listens carefully. Frank traveled to Europe with the military during the Cold War, but he has never been east of Greenville, Kentucky, since then because he hasn't had a reason to. But he has always wondered about New York City. He was Allan's high school teacher in 1961. He sits on the church pew now holding a copy of the high school football magazine from 1968, during the time he was principal. He remembers all the team members by name; he points them out and tells their stories.

Frank tells me just how busy it can get here in the store—how Allan ships thousands of pounds of hog to top chefs in San Francisco and New York every year. But it is Allan's simplicity and honesty, and something about his doe-eyed nature that compel those chefs to make the pilgrimage to Madisonville, to stay at his house and eat his wife Sharon's cooking.

"Quite honestly I almost have to pinch myself because this was a staple for my people," Allan says softly. "If you asked me thirty years ago if even one three-star restaurant would be serving my product, I'd have said not a chance. We count our blessings that chefs like our products, because it's not been many years ago since I thought I was going to starve to death doing this. It's not a way to get rich quick, I'll tell you that. I think a lot of people are making great products across the country. I don't get out enough to see everything that they're doing, but thank God we're beginning to think about where our food comes from. I think that what you eat is important. If I can sell you a ham that doesn't have antibodies, then that's a good thing—for your kids, too. We don't charge any more for it than for regular pork, and I guess in one way I'm not a very shrewd businessman because of that. But I think if you sell your soul for a dollar what have you gained? It's not about who leaves this world with as much dollars in his pocket. It's about making something that you truly can feel good about and are proud of and feel good selling to somebody. That's the bottom line. And if you talk to some of these people who grow vegetables organically I guarantee you that they're pouring their blood and sweat into it for more than a dollar."

As Allan talks, I realize it is not just his hams that people want a part of; it is him. He answers the phone and has unhurried conversations with anyone who calls, regardless of the line trailing out the door. His office is covered with little scraps of paper taped to the wall. That is how he remembers things. His phone is a rotary phone from several decades ago. "It's never had a service call in all that time," he grins. He has been forced to modernize in some ways. He has hired a few men to cure the hundreds of hams and bellies that come in at once and somebody just to handle his shipping. He also has a Gmail account.

"I committed myself to making a good product, to doing it the old way. And I was barely keeping my overhead costs. I work about seventy-five hours per week. I'm cutting it down some. I realize I have to pace myself if I want to last another twenty-five to thirty years. We'd like to quit but we've been doing it since 1947. How do you quit doing something that you've been doing for forty to fifty years? I'm glad people think it's great, but I'm doing no better than my grandparents did in their own backyard. It's a hillbilly operation, and I'm incredibly fortunate that people like what we make. I enjoy what I do. And I've met some very interesting people. And have great employees. Life is good."

He fills a brown paper bag with eight packages of bacon, two packages of ham, two packages of prosciutto, and a three-foot sausage he has spent the past five hours smoking. The sausage is tied with twine and wrapped in gauze casing bearing red glossy letters "Benton's Country Ham." He warns that the sausage and prosciutto wrapping will cause "un-Christian" thoughts and gives me some advice on how to open them.

He hands over the brown bag, hugs me, and tells me to tell my daddy that I have surrogate parents in east Tennessee. If I ever need anything, I am to let him know, because he and Sharon will be there. Then he says softly, "We count our blessings every night, because this happened in spite of us, not because of us."

The parking lot is crammed with Ford and Dodge trucks. Sam Bivins and Randy Watson are loading hams into the back of a van from the loading dock. "We'll be seeing you again!" Randy yells. The van pulls out and disappears up a winding road into the mountain, and I return to the open highway, smelling like salt, smoke, brown sugar, and time.

BENTON'S BACON, LETTUCE, AND TOMATO

From Tellico Grains in Tellico Plains, Tennessee.

BLTs are one of Allan's favorite ways to use his bacon. In Tellico Plains, a few miles from Benton's store, Stuart and Anissa Shull have converted an old bank building into a bakery called Tellico Grains. According to Allan, Tellico Plains is "the only town in the Southeast where you can go on a Saturday and you're still going to see the locals sitting on the tailgates of their trucks in the town square, whittling, chewing tobacco, and swapping lies. It's a piece of Americana that's almost gone." At the bakery, Stuart and Anissa serve a "BBLT," a Benton's bacon lettuce and tomato, on bread that is baked in a brick oven they built themselves. "Your car and clothes smell edible after you leave Benton's," Anissa says. "My daughter says, 'Let's pretend we're going to the bacon store,' when she wants to play."

Herb flatbread roll, split
Aioli (garlic mayonnaise; page 34)
Whole-grain mustard
Benton's smoked bacon, or homemade (page 36)
Cheddar cheese
Tomato
Red onion
Romaine lettuce

Slather the roll with aioli and mustard, and fill with the remaining ingredients.

✒ AIOLI

By now, everyone has mastered the art of putting food between two pieces of bread, so here is a recipe for homemade garlic mayonnaise, which is much better than anything in the store. It is the yellow stuff they dip their french fries in overseas—the kind of thing you can never tire of. You can use all kinds of flavorings in place of the garlic: chopped tarragon or basil, curry powder, or whatever suits your mood.

1 large egg yolk, at room temperature
1 tablespoon Dijon mustard
1 teaspoon Champagne vinegar
Sea salt
¾ cup grapeseed oil or safflower oil
¼ cup good olive oil
2 tablespoons minced garlic (see Note)
Lemon juice, to taste

1. In a heavy bowl (one that you can whisk in without holding on to it), whisk together the egg yolk, mustard, and vinegar. Season with salt.
2. Whisking constantly, add the grapeseed oil in a thin, steady stream, incorporating the oil thoroughly as you go, and not letting it form a pool in the bowl. A glossy custard will form.
3. Whisk in the olive oil (good olive oil is a "finisher"; it gives all things an edge), then fold in the garlic. If you find the mixture has gotten too thick, add a few drops of water and stir.
4. Add the lemon juice to brighten the flavor and more salt as needed. Cover and chill for a few hours to let the garlic permeate the mayonnaise.

Note: A garlic-mincing trick: This is one of the first truly time-saving techniques I ever learned when I decided to get serious about cooking, but for some reason I've never seen it done in professional kitchens. Chop the garlic roughly. Sprinkle a lot of salt on top. Using the flat sides of your knife, press the garlic back and forth over your cutting board the way a mason does with cement and trowel. Within 30 seconds you will have virtually liquid garlic. It is not overwhelmingly salty, as one might expect, and you can simply add less salt to the recipe to compensate.

MAKES ABOUT 1 CUP AIOLI

✒ HOMEMADE BACON

One should always have a relationship with a butcher—the kind who has sawdust on the floors and is willing to talk to you for hours about what you're going to make for dinner. This is a relationship to nurture, because the butcher has the key, the way to gastronomical heaven. Call ahead and ask him or her to order you things, whether you'd like the skin on or off, the bone in or out. Bacon, which comes from the belly of the hog, is easy to make at home. It is most often sold in strips, but when you make it yourself, you can enjoy its true versatility—cut it into batons known as lardons for classic French dishes, or into thicker cubes for soups, stews, and beans, or gently grill a whole slab at once and serve it as the main course. If you want to slice it thinly, freeze it first then use a long slicing knife. Bacon freezes very well because of its high fat content so it is easy to always have on hand. This dry cure recipe can be used to make many kinds of cured meat products, though it works especially well with pork. It can be stored in a plastic container indefinitely and used in a ratio of 50 grams (¼ cup) of the mixture for each 2.25 kilograms (5 pounds) of meat. Variations on the cure include brown sugar or maple syrup for a sweeter bacon, and smashed garlic cloves, cracked black peppercorns, and dried herbs for a savory bacon.

With dry curing, it is best to use weight measurements for all ingredients because it is the most accurate form of measuring, and the path to delicious, safe results. I've provided approximate volume measurements for those without a kitchen scale (which, by the way, is a wonderful tool to have).

> *1.5 to 2.25 kilograms (3 to 5 pounds) pork belly,*
> *   skin on if you plan to smoke it, skin off if you don't*
> *50 grams (¼ cup) dry cure*

Dry Cure:
>   *450 grams (2 cups) kosher salt*
>   *225 grams (1 cup) sugar*
>   *50 grams (10 teaspoons) pink salt #1 (see Note)*

1. Trim the pork belly of any dry meat and glands, and neaten the edges.
2. Combine the salt, sugar, and pink salt. Place the pork belly in a nonreactive baking dish or on a baking sheet covered in plastic, and cover with the mixture, pressing it into all the cracks and crevices. Do this until all sides are evenly and well coated.
3. Place the baking sheet in the refrigerator for 5 to 7 days, turning the pork belly over once a day to make sure it cures evenly, until the meat feels firm throughout. The thicker the belly, the longer it will take to become firm. The pork will release a lot of liquid as it cures, so it is important that the cure stay in contact with the meat the whole time.
4. Rinse the pork belly. Dry it thoroughly.
5. The belly is ready to use. If you want to smoke your bacon, preheat a grill or smoker to 200°F and burn wood chips for at least 30 minutes, then add the bacon. Hot smoke to an internal temperature of 150°F. If you don't own a grill or smoker, you can roast the cured bacon in the oven at 200°F to the same internal temperature. Remove the skin now with a sharp knife while the fat is still hot. It will keep up to two weeks in the refrigerator or you can cut it into manageable sizes, wrap it in plastic, and store it in the freezer for several months.

Note: Also referred to as Prague powder, tinted cure mix, or Insta Cure #1, pink curing salt #1 (a mixture of salt and nitrite) is used in many types of cured meat products that are made and then cooked or eaten fairly quickly. The nitrite keeps the meat safe for a short period of time, and maintains the meat's red color as well as gives it that "cured" taste. Its main purpose is to prevent botulism poisoning. It can be bought from many places on the Internet, or ask your local butcher.

MAKES ABOUT 1.25 TO 2 KILOGRAMS (2 ½ TO 4 POUNDS) BACON

MARION BUSH

The Forager

CHAPTER THREE

Seeing the Forest
for the Fungus

I remember the first time I saw her. I was standing at the bottom of a hill amid the Stone Barns, on the Rockefeller Estate, looking up. She was lifting the trunk of her purple PT Cruiser, surrounded by an audience of strangers. A wiry chef stood next to her clad in a long white apron that matched her fluffy white hair, and he leaned in, picking through her trunk. Something in her nature—a joviality, an innocence—intrigued me. I didn't know who she was or what was in her trunk, but it haunted me until the day I found out. When I did, she became the highlight of the brutal days I spent in a demanding kitchen; she would tell me a quick story and let out a giggle. Marion Bush was a momentary escape from reality.

Marion Bush is a forager of local wild edibles in the lower Hudson Valley who has been known to swerve into the service lane of the Sawmill Parkway in pursuit of a ten-pound hen of the woods mushroom and ardently explain the importance of the fungi in her trunk to a bewildered police officer. She sports T-shirts with slogans like "So many weeds, so little time," and can frequently be found armed with a red backpack and a serious whistle. This means she's ready to hunt.

She lives in Westchester County, New York. She makes a place in her home for every plant and seed she finds. "I am an inveterate after-dinner gardener," she says in a fervent whisper. "And I don't know what all of it is because I put them in pots and say of course I'll remember what they are, but I forget!" Her kitchen is banked with pots filled with the seeds of mangoes, tomatoes, dates, and avocados that she has eaten in evenings past. In the corner of her counter sits a garlic basket that she fashioned out of honeysuckle vines; tacked to the refrigerator is a colored-pencil sketch she drew of her walking iris, which has just bloomed on the windowsill—an event that thrills her. "The flower lasts one day. They rise and then by five-thirty, they close and shrivel. I tried to pollinate them, and the pollen is blue. I've never seen anything like it. I was so excited about the whole thing!"

Outside, her fig tree is still thoroughly wrapped in plastic. She rolls it into the garage during the coldest months. Her garden consists mostly of transplants she has found in the wild. "We plant things and they come up where they want to be. Not where we want them. You never know what's going to happen from one year to the next. It's kind of fun. Sometimes what you planted comes up, sometimes it doesn't."

Marion has an energy that injects anticipation into the air. To walk with her is to walk with the eyes of a child discovering the world for the first time. She exudes an infectious giggle, the kind that makes you feel like you are in on a secret. And Marion has many secrets—not many people know about the sports she has discovered over the years. She is wearing a black sweat suit today because she's just returned from the karate class she attends five days a week. She has done this for the last sixteen years, and is a second-degree black belt. She takes her sensei—her teacher—wild edibles that she finds in the woods and practices karate on construction workers.

She is an ardent advocate of foraging, talks of days gone by when people would forage in their yards for dinner during tough times. She recites stories to me, ones of her great uncle who emigrated from Russia and went out to the woods foraging because food was scarce and expensive. "You went out and you looked for greens, and for mushrooms. People did some hunting where you were allowed to hunt or where you could poach without being caught."

She has areas where she likes to walk. Because she has been doing it for many years, she knows which areas are growing particular plants at a given moment. She used to pick to order. In the days when restaurants valued these ingredients, she had charts so she knew where she could get ramps, and violets, and purslane. For some customers she would say, "Would you like a mesclun mix? Right now this is what I can get, this is what's good." Traditional mesclun, it so happens, is not baby lettuce greens. It is field greens. As she gleefully hops from lambs' quarter to Indian hemp, she surveys the field with a smile and declares, "There is a veritable salad in here!" She tells me tales of the days when she vigorously collected these wild greens. "Oh, I had so much fun. My husband would have co-workers over for dinner and people would admire the collection as a centerpiece. Then we'd put dressing on and eat it."

"There are so many different interesting wild plants that you can eat, and a lot of them people consider weeds. They're growing in your garden, like purslane, and people just throw them out, and they don't know that they're throwing out omega-3s, vitamin C, vitamin E, all sorts of good things. And the flavors are so wonderful. Now we have farmers' markets, but you can't get really fresh stuff in the supermarkets. Things travel for a week. You can taste the freshness, you can taste the difference, and I'd be willing to bet that your body knows the difference too."

Marion learned about foraging from her mother, who gave lectures on wild plants many years ago. A young chef read in the local newspaper about her mother's knowledge of natural edibles and called everyone in the phone book with her surname until he found her. He asked her mother if she would like to supply him. She was taking care of her ill husband and so asked Marion if she would like to start supplying him. "I had no idea what I was doing. I started with one customer. I would tell him what was growing out there and he would tell me how much of it he wanted. And I would pack my daughter and all the greens in the car and drive down to Brooklyn. People would go to the restaurant and eat some of the salads and eat some of the greens and say, 'Oh, where did you get these?' And he'd give them my name and phone number. So back in the eighties I had a lot of customers. And then the boom just sort of slowed down. The restaurant business changed. So little by little, I moved my base of operation here."

She has been foraging for twenty-seven years. After a heart procedure, it was no longer appealing to go down to the city and vie for parking to make deliveries. So now she forages for just one restaurant in Westchester—and, of course, for her sensei.

⸻

It is a late spring, and we are short on rain. I am wearing rubber shoes, poised to thrash through the woods of raining acorns until I find a sea of morels. Marion says this is a hard time of year to identify things unless you really know them. Some people know plants by their bark; she is trying to learn that skill. But she isn't having trouble finding edibles. She is a walking encyclopedia of Latin names. She diverges quickly, mid-sentence, from one discovery to the next, information spouting in all directions in a stream of consciousness. "Oh, this is a trout lily!" It has formed next to "a little vernal pond," which she finds interesting because these ponds form spontaneously in the woods after rain and produce frogs, spring peepers, salamanders, and newts. With a vernal pond comes Japanese skunk cabbage, which, when well boiled (and by that time khaki colored), is considered a "spring tonic" among certain crowds. Then garlic mustard, a non-native brought over in the pant cuffs of English settlers; their tender early leaves make tasty salad. There's sauce-alone, also English, which earned its name because one can make a satisfying sauce from it alone.

Dashing through the woods, we run into smilax, also called blaspheme weed, because you curse when you get caught in it. We do, and she giggles as we peel the briars from our shirts. And then Pennsylvania bittercress, with a rosette shape at the base of its leaves, the appearance of watercress, and the same peppery bitterness. "I can pull them out with impunity because they're everywhere," says Marion, handing me some. This time of year everything tastes very mild, very good.

She points to a carpet of violets, all edible except the yellow ones. "Those will upset your stomach. Guaranteed!" She explains how wineberries differ from raspberries because they don't have the very fine spines on the canes. The fruit, too, instead of being opaque and purple, is translucent and reddish orange, a little bit tarter. She stops mid-sentence again, inhales a short breath. "The cuckoo flowers are open—look at that!" She feeds me the little white, sweet, peppery flowers; a hint of marzipan lingers in my throat. "Oh, this is an interesting one," she says as she moves on. "This is native wild ginger. There are European and Asian ones also, but this is fuzzy, which I love. We get so much ginger from cultivation now that we don't do this anymore, but you can take the roots and candy them."

The woods smell damp and ripe. She kneels to open a parakeet-shaped milkweed pod and describes how she would play with them as a child. She raises her hands and releases a cloud of wispy silk ribbons into the air. Milkweed parachutes into the wind, and for a moment her hair blends with the parachuting silk against the light. "Most people don't have time to really look at the world," she whispers.

She finds a thistle, and pulls out a magnifying glass to see the network of spores. "Sometimes you want to capture and commemorate things," she murmurs. Then she darts away, propels me forward, out of my trance. I can barely follow; she glides through the woods nimbly, prancing over newly fallen trees and vernal ponds. "I just love being out!" She lets out a low, throaty chuckle. There are ferns coming up, and when I catch up to her she is pondering whether they are ostrich ferns. In New York state, all the ferns that taste good are protected by law, so fiddle-heads, the curled fern buds, can be harvested only on private grounds.

"This is spicebush," she continues. "It's an early bloomer. It gets little red berries that dry up and turn black and can be used like allspice." When the colonists arrived, spices from the Far East were so expensive that if you could find an alternative you did. This was an alternative—native, plentiful, local. All you had to do was go out and collect it, then spread the red berries out to dry, then grind them.

"This is a beech tree. The young beech leaves, when they first open, when they're still translucent and very small, are very tasty," she says. The beech is one of the few trees that keeps its leaves over the winter and so is very distinctive in a post-winter woodland. "And they have beechnuts, little triangular nuts they used to use as flavoring for beech-nut gum."

Marion lives in a special universe where unexpected plants in the garden are "volunteering," a wood of falling acorns is called a "hard hat area," where poison ivy is having a "successful year," and a raspberry crop "always races with the frost." From a distance she spots "a whole band of ramps"—little wild leeks. "I sometimes pick just the leaves because that way the bulb is still in the ground and continues to multiply," she says, picking some. This time of year, the white bulb of the ramp hasn't filled with nutrients, so it is relatively thin. In another month they will be large and good for pickling. "A few leaves mixed in with steamed spinach are fabulous," she tells me. "It all adds a little wild flavor to everything. They look so innocuous, they look so lovely and they taste so strongly of leek."

We find sheep's earl and I chew on more garlic mustard, sharply flavored from oxalic acid; there is Japanese barberry, bittersweet, and honeysuckle (good for making baskets), wineberries, heart-shaped wood sorrel, lady's bedstraw (once used to stuff mattresses and thicken milk), more milkweed (where monarch butterflies lay their eggs), horsenettle (a solanine toxic nightshade, with red cherry tomato–like berries), and galancia (which tastes of artichokes).

"There's always more to learn—always," says Marion, petting a ramp, "which is one of the things I love about it. Like karate. The more I know, the more I know there is to learn." She says you can find a lot of plants along ecotones, areas where two different habitats come together. The adjoining area is a very rich natural progression—first are weeds of various sorts, then berries and vines, then trees overshadowing everything.

She gets down into some Japanese nutweed and snaps off a stem that looks like an asparagus. "If you cook this down you could make a wonderful tart sauce; it's like a sorrel sauce, which is fabulous with salmon. The color is just wonderful. These stalks are like bamboo; they grow up tall in one year and then die."

We linger around a dead log to see if any morel mushrooms have sprouted. They occur near burnt wood, old apple trees, and dying elms. After Mount St. Helens erupted, people left with cars full of mushrooms that sprang up in droves from the burnt earth. A man in Marion's karate dojo recently brought her a few mushroom varieties from Virginia that she had never seen before.

To the careless, mushroom hunting is akin to Russian roulette. When Marion was a child, her great uncle had mushroom portraits lined up on his wall. When she asked him which wine he would serve with them, he responded, "A Rothschild 1952." Why such an expensive wine? "Because it will be your last meal," he told her. By the time you start to feel the symptoms of poisonous mushrooms, it is usually too late. "There is a kind of mushroom known as a death cap, or *Amanita velosa*," Marion says. "They are reputed to taste good, and they are lethal."

Mushrooms are a great experiment in dispersal—whether there are blades or spores, facing inward or outward, determines much in a mushroom's life. They are a fruit; like an apple on an apple tree, they grow from a mycelium, a microscopic network of cells. Marion has special places she goes to find mushrooms, and she looks for the conditions that indicate whether she will find them. She watches the moon phases in particular, because mushrooms rely on lunar energy.

In the spring, the wine cap, *Coprinus micaceus*, is the first mushroom to pop up. It does not mix well with alcohol twenty-four hours before or after, so you have to think about what you drank yesterday and what you are going to drink tomorrow when you decide to eat it. Some, like the *Agrocybe praecox* species, appear in early spring in wood chips along with the rough ring *Stropharia rugosoannulata*. "It's like a family: You have to get to know each one," Marion says. In Chinese pharmacopeia, mushrooms are a big variable. Hen of the woods, or maitake, are used to treat types of cancer; tea made from turkey tail mushrooms is used medicinally. "Nature is amazing," she muses. "Many people just see a blur; they don't see all the little parts."

As we make our way out of the woods, Marion tells me how birds get drunk. They wait for grapes and mulberries to ferment and then eat them. A shrieking cloud of birds in a tree is, above all, a drunken wine tasting. "You get these drunken doves staggering around on the street making weird noises to themselves. Oh, they are just so befuddled. You can practically walk right up to them because they are just staggering around going—" and then she lets out a very accurate dove noise.

She points out edible foods as we drive around a Westchester suburb. "After a while your eye gets accustomed to seeing things on the side of the road," she says. "This is a pretty built-up area around here, but it's surprising what you can still find. Plant life is very persistent.

And of course I always have an eye on my neighbors' lawns to see what they're growing. You never know . . ."

She chats with police officers who stop her, mostly wanting to make sure she doesn't eat certain wild plants that are exposed to pollution. "Plants close to the side of the road absorb carbon monoxide. You want to be at least twenty feet back from the side of the road."

In addition to police officers, Marion attracts all kinds of fascinated people, some as interesting as she is. She has a friend who is a venomous insect specialist—the person they call when a truck full of honey bees turns over on the Tappan Zee Bridge.

At a wedding, you will find her educating people—explaining to someone why they should not push the delicious nasturtium flowers to the side of their salad, then stopping them when they start eating the centerpiece, and explaining the difference.

Marion has the ability to see value where most people see weeds. Shortly after I found out who this mysterious woman with special things in her trunk was, I heard someone say, "Marion, you're a genius." Her particular trait is better than genius, though. She has the ability to live a fluid life—to see the forest for the fungus, and the world for its weeds.

✒ PICKLED RAMPS

To live closely to nature is to master the art of eating with the seasons—and also knowing how to preserve those seasons in a glass jar for another day. There are few things more satisfying than dipping into a shelf full of jars whose contents are plum tomatoes, quince jelly, applesauce, and pickled everything—jars you have filled yourself with things you have grown and foraged yourself. This is a basic pickling recipe that can be used with most vegetables. The liquid can be strained and reused many times.

> 1 teaspoon mustard seeds
> 1 teaspoon black peppercorns
> 1 teaspoon fennel seeds
> 1 teaspoon coriander seeds
> 12 cups rice wine vinegar
> 4 cups sugar
> ⅓ cup salt
> Ramps, trimmed of their green leaves
>   (which can then be sautéed fresh)

1. In a large pot over medium heat, toast the spices for several minutes, stirring them constantly until they begin to exude their aroma.
2. Add 4 cups water, the vinegar, sugar, and salt and bring to a boil.
3. Remove the pot from the heat and add the ramps, making sure they're covered with the liquid. Let them sit in the liquid in the refrigerator until you are ready to eat them. If you have a lot of ramps and not a lot of refrigerator, buy a book on canning and fill your shelves with jars for the winter.

MAKES ABOUT 4 QUARTS PICKLING LIQUID

✒ STINGING NETTLE SOUP

Dress yourself in thick rubber gloves and collect stinging nettles. The furry, painful-to-the-touch leaves are distinctive with the help of a good field guide, like *Stalking the Wild Asparagus*, by Euell Gibbons. Though they don't feel nice, they taste nice when treated well. (If you're not feeling adventurous, you can substitute spinach leaves.)

4 quarts stinging nettles
2 tablespoons olive oil
3 onions, sliced paper-thin
2 leeks, white and pale green parts only, thinly sliced
5 cloves garlic, sliced
1 bulb fennel, thinly sliced
2 quarts vegetable stock
Grated zest of 1 lemon
10 fingerling or 4 Yukon gold potatoes, peeled and thinly sliced
Crème fraîche or plain yogurt for serving
Salt and black pepper to taste

1. Bring a large pot of salted water (as salty as the sea) to a rolling boil. Prepare a large bowl of ice water and set it aside. Working in batches, drop the stinging nettles into the boiling water for a few seconds, then remove them with a slotted spoon and transfer them to the ice water. When all of the leaves are blanched and "shocked" in the ice water, remove them from the water, squeeze out the excess water, and set them aside.

2. In a saucepan over medium heat, heat the oil and add the onions, leeks, garlic, and fennel and cook, stirring occasionally, until they are soft, keeping the temperature low enough so that they don't gain a lot of color, about 10 minutes. Deglaze the pan with the stock. Add the lemon zest and potatoes and cook at a low simmer, partially covered, until the potatoes are tender, about 20 minutes. Add the nettles and cook until heated through.

3. Puree the soup in a blender. With a green soup, it is best to cool it as quickly as possible if you are not serving it right away, so it doesn't turn brown. You do this by "shocking" it: Put the soup in a bowl and set the bowl in a larger bowl of ice water. This soup is best served at room temperature, with a dab of crème fraîche or plain yogurt and lemon zest on top.

MAKES 3 QUARTS SOUP

MATTHIAS TRUM

The Brewmeister

CHAPTER FOUR

A Brewmeister
in a Sea of Beer

I t is white asparagus season in Bamberg, Germany. In the Grün Markt, the stalls are teeming with meaty white stalks. The streets exude the smell of sausage and the sound of rubber tires slapping against cobblestone.

The town lies in a basin-shaped valley protected by hills. Two arms of the Regnitz river flow through it. On the streets in the town, everyone says, "*Grüss Gott.*" Colorful fisher houses along the stone bridges make up a kind of little Venice.

Bamberg's history is founded on monasticism and beer. The town formed as a diocese in 972, and it was the home of the Order of St. Benedict in 1015, then the Franciscans in 1223, then the Carmelites in 1273. In the green-and-white half-timbered house past a church is the same monastery started by the Dominicans who arrived in 1310. Above the door to this monastery is a symbol that looks like a star of David, but is actually the oldest gilded trademark from the brotherhood of brewers. Bamberg and the surrounding towns in northern Bavaria have the greatest density of breweries in the world. Together, they represent the beer capital of the universe. In Bamberg alone there are ten breweries, and there are one hundred breweries in the surrounding area, seven hundred in Bavaria.

The first license to brew was granted in 1122, and thereafter hundreds of tiny breweries started up using communally owned brewing vessels that were passed from home to home.

But one brewery in particular, Schlenkerla, has remained in the hands of one family continuously since the fifteenth century. Here they make Rauchbier, a smoked malt beer made with hops dried over an open beechwood fire that produces a brew infused with a smoky aroma and flavor. Miniature copper crosses fill every crevice. Portraits of family members line the walls. In this converted monastery, you are inside and outside at once. There are open-air rooms with staircases leading to the sky; deer heads and antlers adorn the walls above wooden tables teeming with red-faced, round-nosed German men. Painted onto the stucco are the words ingrained in the minds of all the locals: "*Hopfen und Malz, Gott Erhalts!*" (God saves hops and malt).

In the kitchen, dumplings the size of baseballs sit on a tray above a steaming pot of rolling water. "It's important to have some roasted bread inside the dumpling," Wolfgang, the chef, says, splitting one open. Wolfgang drops them into the water after shaping them one last time in his fleshy hands. He has tight red cheeks and is a very merry chef, quite unlike the kind I am used to. And that is reflected in how his food tastes.

Earnest women in black dresses and miniature white frilly aprons—the kind you see at diners in Philadelphia—whisk in and out carrying dimpled platters on their arms. Wolfgang hands me a plate of Kaiserschmarrn, a sliced raisin pancake onto which he shakes copious amounts of powdered sugar. It is a cross between fried dough and dumplings—something you could eat a whole lot of for a very long time.

He tends to his sautéeing kidneys while the apprentice pours beer-flavored gravy over a stuffed Bamberg onion, then sprinkles parsley over a pile of white asparagus. There is no sign of effete portions on over-sized plates here—this is hearty food for hearty people. The apprentice demonstrates how he makes little pork sausages using the same smoked malt they put in their beer. "So our food and our drink taste the same!" Wolfgang exclaims, offering me a bowl of kidneys coated in gravy.

Matthias Trum appears in the doorway. He is the quintessential modern German—young, tall, thin, and blond, with glasses that dance the line between nerdy and cool. He is the sixth generation of his family to run Schlenkerla. His mother handed him this restaurant, known as the brewery tap, in 2007; his father handed him the brewery up the hill in 2003. He runs both by himself, walking up and down the hill between the two to manage them. He has an arsenal of historical facts stored in his brain, interesting ones that weave their way into our conversation effortlessly.

Matthias can tell by looking at the smoke cloud above the brewery on the hill where they are in the brewing process. As we begin to walk up that hill, the smell of beef jerky blows down at us. All along the hill, old sandstone houses are crowned with angular beer chimneys, the kind that directed steam to the sky when, centuries ago, every dwelling produced beer. As we approach the brewery, the smell gets stronger.

Matthias tells me it is the malt roasting against beechwood. A large part of specialty brewing is in the malting. Most big breweries start their process at the malt mill, but when breweries were much smaller they were more involved in every step of the process. Some of them even grew their own grain, and had a brewery tap where they sold the finished product.

With the advent of industrialization, the brewing process was split up into its individual components: the farmer, the grain processing, the malt factory, the brewery. Here Matthias makes beer the old way, controlling most of the process. "A huge part of diversity comes out of making your own malt," he says. "Not just in smoked malt. There are thirteen hundred breweries in Germany, and only fifty malting companies. Malting is much more centralized today. Four or five different brands are using the same malt. If you use the same ingredient you can vary the recipe but you don't have the same variance as if you made your own malt."

Matthias gets his barley from local farmers in the area. He submerges it in water for a few hours, then adds oxygen to help it breathe. Barley is a living organism, and he wants to keep it that way, constantly alternating between water and oxygen so it doesn't suffocate. Then he puts the grain in germination boxes and grows it for four to five days before halting the germination process by smoking it.

The cultivation of grain is inextricably entwined with the development of human civilization. The first humans were able to cease their nomadic ways and start a settled life only because they had discovered how to cultivate grain and then store it by drying. Along with bread, beer is one of the oldest sources of sustenance still being made today. Beer making is said to have begun with the Sumerians and Egyptians, as well as with the high cultures in the Yangtze valley of today's China, all of whom made beer around 7000 B.C. By passing on recipes over centuries, testing them, and comparing results, the process was perfected. Brewers, in effect, were the first biochemists of the world. The ancient Sumerians dried the grain on the roofs of their homes. Here in central Europe that wasn't possible because of rain—the moist, cloudy climate of middle and northern Europe forced brewers to forego the rooftop and smoke green malt over an open fire.

Matthias opens a heavy door and adds beechwood to the smoking kiln, the roof of which is punctured so that smoke permeates the layer of grain above. This wood has always come from Steigerwald, the largest beechwood forest in Germany, ten kilometers west of Bamberg. As coal replaced wood, and industrialization took over, few breweries continued to dry their own local malt. Today modern beer houses use gas or electricity, a kind of blow dryer, which heats the malt without smoking it. This allows them to produce larger, more uniform batches, which is more economical and efficient, though not nearly as tasty. The Trums have kept their own malting facility in place, so today they can still do what other big malt houses cannot: produce small batches of quality smoked malt. "A batch at our house is three and a half tons of malt; one at a modern factory is five hundred tons. So you can see the efficiencies in a larger scale. I can only say that I was lucky that my ancestors were old-fashioned enough and stubborn enough to retain this."

The malt-drying process lasts for a week, then it is brought upstairs to a storage facility. When it is time to brew, malt is mixed with water and called mash. It is heated to 78°C, the temperature at which enzymes produce sugars most successfully. The key to mashing is to make all the elements of the grain soluble. At the end of the mashing process everything that is insoluble is filtered out. Smaller breweries like this one use the gravity system to move their liquid from vat to vat, whereas larger factories use pump systems. Modern methods also use automated filtration pressure systems, which are more efficient, but draw out parts of the grain that have a poor flavor.

In the brewing room, Matthias moves between two shiny copper vats, each puffing steam. The vapors smell of chocolate, and sometimes miso soup. Once this liquid is filtered, only two ingredients are left: malt and water. Then hops, a bitter flower used as a stabilizing agent, is added to the hot liquid and a chain-driven paddle stirs the mixture in the copper vat for two hours.

Through a whirlpool system, the soluble elements assemble in the middle and form a cone. Once cooled, yeast is added, and primary fermentation begins.

In Germany, using a single type of yeast is considered a higher form of brewing. Belgian beers are more complex because they are less pure—they are wild-fermenting beers—open to spontaneous fermentation, using whatever yeast comes in from the air; sometimes ninety strains of yeast occur in a single beer.

Smiling at the particular nature of his brewing culture, Matthias says, "A German brewer would not do that; it's part of our brewing pride." The whole notion of yeast strains is a fairly modern concept that was unknown in previous centuries of beer making.

The experience and skill of the brewer come in to play when dealing with the yeast—how long you ferment, at what temperature, using what raw materials; every batch is slightly different. "Modern life is pretty much soaked up by technology," Matthias says, opening the door to a long, steep staircase. "Every aspect of what you do has some technical background to it. You have computers running your life, you have chemical analysis. But brewing is still very much about humans and history."

The smell of wet cement thickens the air as we go down the stairs into Bamberg's "seven hills"—an intricate system of tunnels and caves that render the hills of the town a veritable Swiss cheese. In the Middle Ages, people used these tunnels to store food by harvesting ice and carrying it below. During World War II, there were factories down here, bomb shelters, churches, storage facilities, and living areas. There was a time when people lived most of their lives in the caves and tunnels of Bamberg. If you can find the way through this pitch-black maze, you can access almost every house in Bamberg from underground.

When artificial cooling became popular, many breweries closed their caves and built lagering (storing) facilities close to their breweries. The Trums went the opposite way and put their brewery on top of their lagering caves and were eventually able to buy surrounding houses along with the cellars underneath them, thus extending their lagering capacity.

"I'm quite happy that we have enough space to actually still be able to do that," Matthias says as he moves deeper into the darkness. "It creates a more multilayered and complex taste as the esters develop (esters are the compounds that give beer a fruity, sometimes banana flavor). And I'm making use of Bamberg's underground tunnels." Lagering and maturation takes two months for his classic beer. Larger brewers like Budweiser will rarely take this step because it costs money and time. After lagering, the beer is filtered to take out the remaining yeast, then put into barrels and eventually into bottles.

A man in rubber overalls washes stacks of oak barrels and charming little kegs. The barrels have to stay moist in order to properly store the beer. Once filled, they are brought into the caves and twice a week go down the hill to the brewery tap. Because it isn't pasteurized, the beer lasts one month in these wooden barrels, as opposed to four to six in a commercial metal barrel. But the family still uses wooden barrels because they best preserve the flavor.

⁓

We ascend back into the sunlight and down the hill. Everyone knows Matthias—he waves as he walks, complimenting the local antiques dealer on his pink tie, saluting his uncle in the beer garden. Someone once told me to look up when I walk because it makes you feel more optimistic. Bamberg is the place to try this. Lots of little Virgin Marys and concubines are tucked away in stone corners. Behind the densely packed houses are hidden gardens.

At the entrance to the tap, an elderly German man is gazing over a pint of beer onto the streets, a silver Husky lying at his feet. We sit behind him in the seven-hundred-year-old chapel of the Dominican monastery—low Gothic ceilings, cozy and narrow; an old tile oven at the end of the room, shiny and scrubbed, the devout scourings of six centuries. Portraits of the bishops of Bamberg peer down at us, as they once observed the monks who sat here for daily prayer. Little has changed here in seven centuries. The kettles and the pokers, the oxblood-stained beams, and the drink all remain as they were.

For centuries, the church was a place where the devoted could learn a craft and hone it. And at Schlenkerla, in a harmonious alternation of prayer, study, and work, the monks made some of the world's finest beer— the ultimate expression of men choosing a simple life and honest manual labor. Monasteries had uncompetitively low prices, and could produce a religiously brewed beer that was cheaper than anywhere else. "So," Matthias says, "if you were to buy their beer, the monks had the better beer, it was cheaper, and you did something good for your afterlife!"

Matthias's ancestors, who eventually took the brewery over from the monks, look down at us now, their lacquered faces pleasantly framed in mahogany. Like the European monarchies, the Bamberg breweries formed dynasties, with children intermarrying—merging and acquiring—to form new breweries. In Matthias's family can be found connections to at least ten earlier breweries. "That's what I like so much about the business," Matthias says, sitting at the end of the wooden table observing the room. "When I look at the line of my ancestors I can see, for every generation, what they did and what their contribution was. There is a picture of each of them hanging in the tavern. Like in Scottish castles you have the old dukes and earls on the wall, I have the old brewers up there. This one built the new bottling line, this one bought that house. Looking to the future, it gives me optimism. I hope that one day my offspring will look at my picture and know what I did. It kind of makes you feel you live on after you leave the planet. We've been doing what we do for six hundred years. A lot of people lack that tradition these days. When you work for a big company, you have your inbox and your outbox and you don't have a connection to what you're doing or to the past."

Even in this part of Germany, where time seemingly stands still, tradition is eroding a bit. In the twelfth century, Bamberg was referred to as Caput Mundi—Latin for "world capital," but today the city is deprived of people—there are a lot of students, but not a lot of developing families. Industrialization never took place here: no coal mines, no steel. Historically, Bavarians were poor, which is why they plowed their own fields and tended their own farms—and had their microbreweries. Out of that poverty came the rich diversity of brews they have today. And even though farming areas are experiencing a renaissance, young people continue to leave the small towns. "Quite a few of those traditional places have disappeared in the past few years," Matthias says. "That is a problem, in my opinion, a serious one. Young people want to be in cities rather than carry on their parents's business."

This is a particular problem with a product like beer. "Really small, handcraft breweries don't have the shelf life to export. You're expected to drink it in a week. They're not preserved, they're not filtered beyond belief. If they were to export, the beers would lose their interesting taste." Smoked beer is one of the only ways to catch a glimpse of that traditional taste because smoke is a natural preservative, which means the beer can travel greater distances. But the flavor is still quite different at the source. Matthias vaguely remembers the days in the 1970s when people sent their children to pick up pitchers of beer. The children took their share and then made up the difference from the neighborhood fountain before they took the pitchers home.

As plates of Franconian knuckle in beer sauce, smoked malt sausage, and a salad of fluffy white radish descend upon our table, Matthias talks about his holidays and vacations as a child when he had to peel potatoes in the kitchen. "My grandmother was extremely down to earth. She just served potatoes and meat, the traditional foods that go best with the beer, in my opinion. But back in the nineteen twenties, my great-grandmother was making very classic cuisine, even mussels. They say winters used to be colder here so the food was heartier. This kind of food has a lot to offer." He calls the food tradition "very stubborn": his older compatriots won't serve ice cream, cake, Coke, coffee, French fries, ketchup—"it's very un-Americanized."

"But all the children want to go to McDonald's these days. They don't even know the old stuff anymore. The traditional dish for children was a dumpling with a little bit of gravy. And once they're given that, most children actually like it. We're quite particular about this old stuff."

An enormous pig shank is before me, and I am having a hard time paying attention. There is a bowl of beige sauerkraut next to it, enough for four people. Our serious waitress returns with pints of beer, the dark classic smoked beer and the light wheat beer, cool and wonderful to drink. Switching between pig and beer, I savor the flavor and aroma of the chestnut-colored drink, the sweetness from the malt infused with the smell of a campfire, bacon, and tobacco. I pause between sips, alternating with the crisp pork skin and braised meat and allow my taste buds to recover; the longer I take between sips, the more I taste the smoke. What is remarkable is that the wheat beer doesn't have any smoked malt in it. It has merely picked up the aroma from being in the presence of the brewing system.

The wooden barrel also adds to the smokiness. Here in Bavaria, men in leather aprons hammer the spouts in manually at just the right rate so the beer doesn't explode. The modern draft system uses a pump, which requires carbon dioxide, pressured air, or nitrogen, which alters the pure flavor of the beer. This modern draft system will allow beer to sit for several days, which is why the wooden barrel draft method is almost extinct. Here, the wooden barrel at the bar flows through natural gravity, producing an unaffected taste. This is the freshest beer you can get; it has to be consumed within two hours, before it gets warm.

In the whole brewing process there are thousands of variables, as the portfolio of grain and other raw materials constantly change. The art of brewing lies in getting each batch of beer to taste close to the same at the end of the procedure, despite their different starting points. "The idea of vintages is appalling to traditionalists," Matthias says. "Here people often drink their beer out of patriotism. They adapt to the flavor of their local beer. These people are raised by the bottle. They are devoted to their local beer regardless of whether there's a better one twenty miles away. If it changes, they will notice."

Because of this flavor loyalty, a place like Schlenkerla, which makes fourteen thousand hectoliters a year, can compete with a company like Budweiser, which makes 500 million hectoliters a year. Though modern life is full of technology, it is still the taste buds of the brewmaster that determine the quality of the final product.

"There are all kinds of variables I can measure, but how it will taste, no computer can tell me," Matthias says, crunching on snowy radishes. "In that respect, food is so interesting in the modern world because you have the technical approach, which gives certainty, but still you have that artisanal, artistic approach, which you can only take as a brew master and that gives you something else. It's a very unique line of work. Some things you can't learn in school, only by experience. It's about what happens on your tongue. Technology only gets us so far; the final edge is the human factor. A good example is Stradavarius violins. Even by today's standards they're still considered to be some of the best violins ever made. Wouldn't one figure that with computers and modern acoustics and all we know about physics it would be possible to build a better violin today? But it isn't. It's pretty much the same with beer; it's been around for millennia. You can enhance the old recipes here and there and maybe get certain efficiencies tweaked by a computer or by using a truck to transport it rather than a horse-drawn carriage. But the soul of the beer is the history and tradition that's behind it, the old recipe. You just can't take out the human factor."

Matthias has discovered that the perfect time for tasting beer, or anything else, is 11 A.M. After breakfast, the palate has cleared and is most receptive to nuances in taste. After lunch, at 3 or 4 P.M., he doesn't notice flavor variations as much. These are the kinds of things you discover when your work and life are focused on your product and blend into a satisfying existence. "I did other internships in other fields, and as soon as I left the office after eight or nine hours my mind wandered to other things. Here every thought revolves around what I'm doing. Because I'm really interested in what I'm doing."

In high school, he was the only one in his class not to go to job counseling, something for which he is grateful. "I couldn't have hit it much better," he says, forking the last morsel of smoked sausage from his plate. "I love history, I love to be my own boss, to decide for myself what I do. If I make a decision I can follow through on it the next day and not have to run through three lines of bosses to get permission . . . I get to see the ideas come alive. And, most important, I have roots.

If you build up your own business like Bill Gates did that's of course amazing, economically, and scientifically. But one thing he'll never have is history behind that. Will people always use his computers? I don't know. But people will always drink beer. In my line of work I can say, 'Well, we've been around for six hundred years.' It gives me closure in life and it helps me know where I came from and where I'm going to go."

On this night, armed with a package of smoked chocolates, looking up at a dozen Virgin Mary statuettes, I get lost in the pious cobblestone streets of Bamberg, wet and shiny in the evening drizzle. In a world where the brand image has become more important than the quality of the product, I have discovered a place where simple hard work and centuries of tradition have produced exquisite success.

✌ FRANCONIAN BEER KNUCKLE

Adapted from Chef Wolfgang, a merry man in Bamberg, Germany.

There is something soulful about this breed of food, something intensely nourishing. Wolfgang recommends serving salad and baked potatoes on the side.

> *1 pound vegetables: carrots, leeks, celery, and onions*
> > *(in roughly equal amounts)*
> *4 pork shanks*
> *Salt and black pepper*
> *1 tablespoon ground caraway*
> *1 tablespoon oil*
> *1 tablespoon butter*
> *1 tablespoon flour*
> *1 cup Schlenkerla Rauchbier (Schlenkerla smoked beer)*

1. Preheat the oven to 400°F.
2. Roughly dice the vegetables. Rub the pork shanks well with salt and pepper and "spice it lightly," as Wolfgang says, with the ground caraway. Heat the oil in a heavy casserole or Dutch oven over medium-high heat and brown the shanks on all sides. Add the vegetables and cook, turning, until browned. Add enough water to partially cover the shanks and vegetables, then put the lid on and transfer to the oven. Roast for 2 hours.
3. Ladle 1 cup of the liquid from the casserole into a cup or bowl and set aside. Turn the shanks skin side up. Return to the oven to roast, uncovered, for another 20 minutes, until the shanks are crisp on top.
4. Meanwhile, melt the butter in a medium saucepan and whisk in the flour. Whisk in the reserved roasting liquid. Bring to a simmer and cook, whisking all the while, for about 3 minutes. Add the beer and simmer and whisk a few minutes more. The sauce will be thin. Serve the shanks on a platter with the sauce poured on top.

MAKES 4 LOVELY FALL-OFF-THE-BONE SHANKS

✒ BAMBERG STUFFED ONIONS

Bamberg has special onions. They are very large, very round, and very white. They are rich and powerfully strange things. You may have to buy a Vidalia onion or the like if you don't have time to pick one up from Bamberg. Wolfgang tells me that Bamberg stuffed onions are served with mashed or boiled potatoes.

4 large white or Vidalia onions
4 slices smoked bacon, diced
¼ pound ground pork
2 large eggs
1 cup bread crumbs
1 teaspoon freshly grated nutmeg
1 teaspoon dried marjoram
4 tablespoons chopped fresh parsley
1 teaspoon salt
1 teaspoon freshly ground black pepper
2 tablespoons flour
2 tablespoons beef stock or water
1 cup Schlenkerla Rauchbier (Schlenkerla smoked beer)

1. Preheat the oven to 375°F.
2. Peel the onions. Cut about 1 inch off the top of each and reserve it, then cut ½ inch off the other end to create a flat surface for the onion to sit upright. From the top end, scoop out the insides with a spoon until the sides are about ¼ inch thick; set the shells aside.
3. Finely dice the insides of the onions and sauté them in a skillet with the bacon until soft, about 5 minutes.
4. Let cool for a few minutes, then combine the cooked onions and bacon with the pork, eggs, bread crumbs, nutmeg, marjoram, and parsley in a large bowl; season with salt and pepper.
5. Fill the 4 onion shells and set them upright in a baking dish and pour in water to ¼ of an inch. Roast, uncovered, for about 45 minutes, until tender and cooked through, adding the reserved onion tops to the onions halfway through the roasting time.

6. Remove the onions to a platter and pour the pan drippings into a small saucepan. Place over medium heat and whisk in the flour, then the stock and beer. Simmer and whisk until the gravy thickens.

MAKES 4 STUFFED ONIONS

<hr>

⚘ HOMEMADE SAUERKRAUT

You can use any kind of cabbage for this recipe, but if you mix red and green cabbage you will end up with a nice pink sauerkraut. You can start a new batch before the previous batch runs out by using what remains from the crock, repacking it with fresh salted cabbage, and pouring the old juices over the new. This will act as an active starter culture and give your new batch a "boost." If you develop a rhythm like this you will always have sauerkraut on hand.

Caraway seeds, juniper berries, or even other vegetables can be added to the cabbage for flavoring. This is your chance to experiment. To serve warm, you can heat it in equal parts brining liquid and vegetable or chicken stock for 20 to 30 minutes.

5 pounds cabbage
3 tablespoons sea salt
Caraway seeds, juniper berries, or any flavoring you want to try

1. Chop or grate the cabbage finely or coarsely, however you prefer. Put the cabbage in a large bowl, sprinkling it with the salt as you go. This draws moisture out of the cabbage and creates the brine in which the cabbage will ferment. The amount of salt does not need to be precise: In warmer temperatures you might need more, in cooler temperatures less.

2. Add the caraway or other flavorings to the cabbage and toss to combine. Pack a small amount at a time into a 1-gallon or larger ceramic crock or food-grade plastic bucket, pressing down as you go to help release the water from the cabbage. Cover the cabbage with a plate or other flat object that fits snugly into the crock. Place a jug of water or other weight on top of the plate to add pressure. This will help release more water over time. Cover the crock with a cloth or towel to keep ambient dust and flies away.

3. Press down on the cabbage periodically over the next 24 hours until the brine rises above the plate. Some cabbage, particularly if it is old, contains less water. If the brine does not rise above the plate after 24 hours, simply add enough salt water (in a ratio of 1 teaspoon salt dissolved in 1 cup water) to bring the level above the plate.

4. Let the cabbage ferment, and check it every few days to make sure the water level is still above the plate. Keeping it in a cool place will slow the fermentation, and preserve the kraut longer. The volume reduces over time and a "bloom" may appear at the surface. This is simply a reaction to contact with air and can be skimmed off.

5. The kraut will become tangy after a few days and will become stronger over time. In cool temperatures it will keep improving for months. Take it from the crock to eat as needed, but leave the rest in the crock, fully submerged, to continue to develop. If you find that the brine evaporates over time, just add more salt water.

MAKES 1 GALLON KRAUT

MARC BUZZIO

The Salami Soldier

Fighting for Salami

O n a New York City street corner, construction workers with round bellies and long white beards work their jack-hammers at a thunder pitch. The musty smells of sawn lumber and wet cement is a familiar pleasure. A black man with some sort of cape has hitched a ride on the back of a woman's electric wheelchair, scooting with élan down Eighth Avenue. Inside an overlooked storefront at the corner of Twenty-Ninth Street, the walls are white-tiled in the Italian fashion. Dark-cured pork belly, large and small sausages, and macerating peppers are stacked in a cooler beside oozing platters of baked ziti. Marc Buzzio, a squat salami maker with a handlebar mustache and a wide reputation, holds a *cacciatorini*, a small hand-tied salami, and says resolutely, "This is how I judge a person's ability to make charcuterie." He tells me how he cures the marbled shoulder of the heritage pork he buys from a farmers' co-op in Iowa. Marc buys animals according to what he is going to make with them—the British Tamworth pig for its fat belly, the Berkshire for its marbling, the Hungarian Mangalica just to experiment, because any pig that is as hairy as a sheep is worth investigating.

Five thousand miles away is a house with thick stone walls in the village of Curino, near Biella, Piedmont. It is the house that Marc's late father, Ugo Buzzio, lived in. As a young man, Ugo apprenticed under the village's charcuterie maker, Mario Fiorio. They lived on opposite ends of the hill. The air in that part of the world was what made it special—where the Alps are all that separates Italy from France and there is no discernible line between French and Piedmontese charcuterie. There Ugo learned how to make *pâté de campagne*, sopressata, pepperoni, *saucisson à l'ail, cacciatorini*, merguez, bresaola, *cotto*, mortadella—anything that could be made with wine, salt, spices, and beautiful meat and hung to dry in a natural casing. He also made lardo, prosciutto, pancetta, cured belly, and guanciale—simple raw meat coated and dried in the open air. Mario and Ugo were guided by their senses—taste, smell, look, touch. That was how they did it.

In 1930 Ugo got a job at a charcutier in New York City, one that had opened five years earlier and later came to be known as Salumeria Biellese. In the years that passed, Ugo made very few changes, except to add more influence from his roots. Then in 1962 he got a call from Piero, the eighteen-year-old son of the man under whom he had apprenticed in Italy. Ugo gave him a job at Salumeria Biellese, where Piero went on to work twelve hours a day, making charcuterie the way his father had made it in Curino. Piero's son-in-law, Paul, eventually joined, and today works alongside Ugo's son Marc.

Marc still owns the house in Curino. He has kept the old and added new features, alarming villagers with novelties like central air conditioning. This is how Marc has approached his life as one of the last makers of traditional dry-cured charcuterie in the United States.

───

In the summer of 2002 new United States Department of Agriculture regulations emerged for dry-aged ready-to-eat products. "They had egg on their face," says Marc, after events like the "mad cow" outbreak. The regulations were written with industrial producers like Hormel and Boar's Head in mind, not mom-and-pop stores. The USDA told producers they had to prove that their products were safe by showing that they met lethality standards for *Listeria monocytogenes* and *E. coli*—meaning that at the time they were sold, their curing process made it impossible for those bacteria to survive.

While at first it seemed simple, the USDA offered little guidance other than the vague statement that producers of aged meat were going to have to define what made their products safe. And the USDA would then decide if that constituted "proof." Making cured sausages the same way Marc's father did, the way others have for hundreds of years, didn't constitute proof. Neither did the fact that no one has ever gotten sick from his product, or that he uses only heirloom pork and tends to his salamis with the care devoted to a newborn. It wasn't even proof that the USDA itself had tested his shop's product and found it negative for bacteria every year since 1928. The USDA only cared about the process. The traditional method—raw meat, salt, spices, and a lot of time transformed into an edible product was something they couldn't explain, and it made them very nervous, so they offered Marc three options. He could heat the product to a certain temperature, which would cook it, he could irradiate it, or he could add chemicals and preservatives. "I chose none of those," he says, raising his middle finger. "This is what I said instead."

Because larger producers are already using a "kill step," and because they had in-house scientists and powerful lobbyists, it was easy for them to prove that their products met lethality standards. They were proceeding on a well-trodden path. But no one had ever beaten a path for artisanal makers of dry-cured charcuterie. It was coercive for small producers—they didn't have to use a kill step, but if they didn't the USDA offered no way for them to prove their process was safe.

And so New York went from 140 cured meat and sausage producers to 40 between 2001 and 2005. Those that remained were companies like the hot dog maker Sabrett; those that disappeared were small operators who didn't have the means to fight—all except Marc Buzzio, who was prepared to go to war.

He called one of his customers, who was in the agricultural department at Cornell University, and asked him for advice. He wondered how he was to conduct a certified scientific study of the Buzzio family recipes without revealing the Buzzio family recipes. Marc's customer directed him to the scientists in Chicago that the USDA used to develop its rules; the idea was that the USDA wouldn't question its own scientists. The scientists flew to New York, and Marc hired them. They agreed to test the Buzzio family recipes that Ugo had written phonetically in a black book decades ago, and they agreed to keep the recipes secret.

Meanwhile, in 2003, the USDA told Marc he could no longer sell his charcuterie. Closing the doors of Salumeria Biellese meant unraveling the tie between a Manhattan street corner and a hillside village in the Italian Alps. So Marc fought further, and demanded he be allowed to "hold and test" each batch of cured meat—if each batch was tested in a laboratory and found safe, he could sell it to his customers. The USDA, under legal pressure, relented and allowed him to reopen his doors under those conditions.

In the end, the team of Chicago scientists penned a report that confirmed what centuries of practice had already shown—that the traditional method of dry-curing charcuterie was safe for consumption. The scientists had followed Salumeria Biellese's process to the letter, then took it one step further: they injected each product with pure *E. coli* and *L. monocytogenes*, producing much higher levels of bacteria than would normally be found in raw meat. Then they aged the products in the same way they were aged at the salumeria. When the scientists tested the meats at the end of the aging period, the bacteria was gone. They referred to this as a "phenomenon," a word that Marc says is hard for USDA inspectors to consider. "We are a headache to the USDA because we are doing something that scientifically they still can't figure out. They don't understand why the procedure works, but it does. It's not scientific to us; it's a matter of centuries of doing the same thing the same way—it works." New inspectors go through six weeks of training that Marc sees every day is insufficient. "The self-policing system they have implemented for meat producers doesn't work. They are driven by fear and they only see in black and white; there's never a gray area."

Eventually, once presented with this report, once Marc had spent $100,000, the USDA accepted his findings as proof. This was the first time a path had been carved for small artisanal producers of charcuterie. He knows that many salami makers do not have the means to defend themselves and find it easier to close up shop; no artisan lobbyists walk the glossy halls of Washington. Traditional products will disappear, and large producers, who have lobbyists and Congress in their corner, will lose their competition. And consumers will lose the rare taste of things done well.

———

I sit at a table in Marc and Paul's restaurant, Biricchino, attached to the corner deli, fawning over plates of meat and cheese, and dainty peppers; excavating a tiramisù. Customers adorned in gold chains order plates of hand-cut pasta, braised rabbit, and ample Chianti. Marc and Paul are like caricatures, Mario and Luigi, animated and gesticulating, cracking jokes about the days when they were under the watchful eyes of the patriarchs, Ugo and Piero. Paul traces the contours of mountains in the air, depicting the spice mounds his father-in-law always made on the counter before he cured his meats. "You don't measure, you taste," he says. "He could tell by looking at the meat and the amount of fat on it how much spice it would need. He knew if the spices that came in were milder than normal. He could tell which one of his employees had made the salami by tasting it."

It was Ugo and Piero's resistance to change that carried Marc and Paul to their superlative place in history. Whenever they suggested something new they were met with the ultimate insult, "*Ma va*" (Get out of here).

Marc says how much the USDA inspectors have changed from the old days. Once they were knowledgeable; today they "look at the paper-work, not the product. They are more concerned with litigation than what goes into the sausages," he says.

He recalls how a new inspector, fresh out of training, arrived one morning visibly white and anxious and quietly informed him that she was going to have to shut him down. She leaned in and told him he had mold growing on his sausages. He spent the next twenty-four hours helping her do Internet research to understand that bacteria is part of the process. He educated her in a way the USDA had not. Where once there were old timers who understood the meat business, today Marc has set aside hours of his time to teach new inspectors how to do long division and calculate averages, when he would rather be making salamis.

"You could put a block of Velveeta cheese on Eighth Avenue in August and come back in September and it would be the same. It would kill any bacteria that came around it. It is shelf stable, and that's what they are comfortable with," Marc says, hands in the air. "If a child spends his life eating Velveeta and processed foods and then one day finds himself sitting in Tivoli, France, with a beautiful glass of wine and beautiful bread and the waiter comes out with a stunning Époisses cheese and he gets sick, it is because we haven't exposed him to natural amounts of bacteria." Paul leans back in his chair and says earnestly, "If you spend your life eating sterile foods, you will get sick from bacteria. If you expose yourself to moderate amounts of it, you won't."

———

I amble through the shop in a white lab coat and baseball hat. There is a USDA inspector lurking in rooms with aging sausages. It is a strange juxtaposition, against a pile of glistening hog jowl that sits on the sink waiting to be washed, destined for *guanciale* (cured jowl). I remember reading once that the well-exercised hog jowl is sometimes thought to be better flavored than the belly. Looking at them, I can taste the sweetness of rendered *guanciale*. Then walking into the closet of sausages for the first time I feel strangely nostalgic. It has a particular smell of elegant rot that testifies to centuries of practice. The sweet aroma is comforting; it is the smell of tradition.

Dry curing is a slowly maturing sequence of events, a waltz among protein, moisture, oxygen, and warmth, that, when done well, eliminates harmful bacteria and nourishes beneficial ones. The art is in finding that delicate balance of ideal conditions in which raw meat ages properly, much in the same way conditions are needed for wine and cheese to reach their consummate state.

In the right room, like the eighty-year-old drying room at Salumeria Biellese, the atmosphere is rich in *Lactobacillus*, the bacteria that creates acidic air and prevents harmful bacteria. It is a balancing act that has been passed down through generations of the Buzzio family, since

Ugo first smuggled the bacteria into the United States via sausages from Italy. In the salumeria's new facility in Hackensack, New Jersey, salami makers introduce sausages from the New York City drying room and rotate them in and out, the bacteria slowly forming, rotating, and improving the environment. Marc runs his finger across lines of green and white mold, a sign that the balance is getting better though not quite there. Soon, the mold will be all white. He places his hands around two *coppa*, whole dry-cured pork neck, and can feel a difference that I can't, that one is softer than the other. It is a skill that relies on experienced senses in place of precise quality control.

"This is what I'm passionate about," he says, opening a box of heritage pork shoulder. He flips it over so I can see all sides and marvel at the marbling. He pets it, he ogles it. The fat is bright white and thick—a perfect specimen to be transformed into sausage. He relishes the idea of choosing a breed of pig and using it for its special traits. He believes that is what nature intended. He likes talking to the supplier who sends his pigs out into the woods where they feed on hickory nuts. He is tickled when he learns it is the year of the seven-year locusts and the pigs are chasing them down, which will probably change the flavor of his meat. When farmers have a pig that they feel especially attached to, they call Marc because they know that he will honor the pig by doing something special with it. "Every piece of pork is different," he says. "You have to treat it differently by looking at it. The goal is not to have one single flavor predominate. If you taste garlic or thyme or whatever, it is masking the flavor of the meat."

Because the USDA allows only a certain number of hair follicles per square inch on meat, to save time commercial producers skip over all of the unique breeds and only use white-haired pigs because their hair follicles cannot be counted, eliminating a range of flavor in the process. The meat is treated differently too. Commodity pork parts of unknown origins arrive in large four-cubic-foot frozen blocks. The blocks are dumped in a separator with the seasonings, ground up, and churned before the meat is pushed through a metal worm into artificial casings and sealed with metal clips. No one looks to see what's inside that block of frozen meat. No one knows where all of those parts came from or whether some were of poor quality. No one bothers to take the green gland that causes bitterness out of the shoulder meat. The sausages are then irradiated or cooked, and sprayed with rice flour to give them the appearance of age. "The irony is that if you hang one of those irradiated sausages up the way they do on Arthur Avenue in the Bronx, you actually are opening yourself up to a host of bacteria," Marc says. "That is why most salami packages tell you to keep them refrigerated."

The machines Marc uses are simple ones. Human hands are always at work, and at the end is a rack of hundreds of dangling mini *cacciatorini*. They are delicate and labor intensive, fed manually through a hydraulic sausage stuffer into pork casings. Some of the casings burst, which is typical for natural casings, especially with smaller sausages. It is about feeling the right balance of pressure with your hands as you stuff the casing, knowing when to stop, and knowing when to push just a little bit further. Three men stand around a metal table with spools of twine in their hands and perform the intricate cat's cradle to tie them. The hand tying takes years to learn. It was years before Marc was allowed to tie the *cacciatorini*. Every day Ugo gave him a soft pine dowel and a length of string and instructed him to tie knots around the dowel without making a dent in the wood. Marc tied the knots as gently as he could, but when his father untied them, he found tiny impressions in the wood, or found that the knot wasn't tight enough so that air would get into the salami and prevent it from aging well. After two years, Marc was allowed to tie the larger salamis, and from there he worked his way up the sausage chain to the *cacciatorini*.

The moisture from the diminutive sausages drips to the floor in a pink puddle for twenty-four hours before it is rolled into the delicate curing room. As Marc unwraps a *finocchiona*, a fennel-infused salami, he explains that a good salami has an even texture on the outside and inside, not the hard outer casing and the undercured inner part that is common. To produce *finocchiona*, he buys beef casings from Spain that are hand-stitched in three parts. Natural casings can breathe, he says, which develops the bacteria. Marc experiments with natural casings, adjusting the diameter according to how finely the meat is ground, while the flow of oxygen tunes the flavor harmony.

We return to the curing room, which hovers at a constant 55°F; the low temperature and humidity are controlling the bacterial balance and prolonging the aging process. He caresses the large *coppas* made from Ossabaw pig, a breed native to Ossabaw Island off the coast of Georgia. They are almost ready. He takes down the smallest one and begins to shave thin slices from it. He holds them up to the light so I can see through them. I taste the mild sweetness, the pure tang of pork, and the afterthought of secret spices. This is the taste of waiting.

Then he opens a *fellino*, a skinny pink salami speckled with brunette peppercorns; it is buttery, round, and delicate—no acid, no chemical aftertaste. I can almost identify one particular flavor but then I can't, a maddening game of cat and mouse between my palate and my brain. Therein lies the art of salami, what makes it seductive, what makes you keep eating more.

This culinary art came from necessity. For centuries, curing meat was the way poor people lived off the land during the winter months. The natural phenomenon is a gift of nature that scientists don't understand and the USDA fears. Marc Buzzio embraces it, and carries it forward to a place of perfect proportion with the modern age. He composes in a year what a commercial producer makes in a day. And though he plans to expand, he is not going to grow beyond the point where he cannot maintain his tradition. His mother always told him he had to go to school; he certainly never thought he would go into the family business. "I was having a good time as a teacher. Then my father asked me if I was ready to get serious." After spending a summer with his father working in charcuterie, he never looked back. "My job is my passion and it is fun," he says to me, smiling beneath the brim of his lavish mustache. And his education turned out to be useful in the dry-cured charcuterie business after all, because it helped him fight the government and win.

There are only a handful of people left in the country who are doing anything close to what Marc and Paul are doing, and most of them use a starter culture. They don't have access to bacteria that was smuggled in from Italy in the early twentieth century or the devotion to preserving a centuries-long tradition of good flavor. This is a salami worth fighting for.

✒ LONZA

Lonza means "loin," and refers to an air-cured pork loin. Traditionally, *lonza* is prepared with the meat beginning at the neck of the pig, down to the fifth rib, whereas *lonzino* is made with the meat from the sixth rib down. I have vivid memories of sitting in the Arkansas delta beside a lake, or on a hunting preserve, eating slices of *lonza* made by the local Italian immigrants. It tastes delicate and mild, similar to prosciutto but not quite as rich. It is best eaten on its own so you can taste all the subtleties of the pork and spices. I recommend buying from a quality, even heritage breed supplier since you will really notice a lesser quality pork in this recipe.

> 1 2-kilogram (4-pound) pork loin
> 70 grams (½ cup) kosher salt
> 20 grams (2 tablespoons) sugar
> 5 grams (1 teaspoon) pink salt #2 (see Note)
> 10 grams (2 teaspoons) ground black pepper
> 5 grams (1 teaspoon) ground white pepper
> 5 grams (1 teaspoon) ground cloves
> 12 grams (2 teaspoons) fennel seeds
> 16 grams (1 teaspoon) mixed dried herbs
>   such as marjoram and thyme

1. Trim the loin of excess fat and neaten the edges.
2. Combine the salt, sugar, pink salt, and spices and herbs. Rub the mixture all over the loin, massaging it thoroughly into the meat. Put the loin in a resealable plastic bag or wrap it well in plastic and put it in the refrigerator for 10 to 12 days until it looks darker and feels firmer.

3. Remove from the refrigerator and let air dry on a rack for 3 to 5 hours. Truss the loin with kitchen twine, looping, pulling the string through, and looping again, the way you would a roast (leaving extra string at the end for hanging the loin). This gives the loin a uniform shape and even cure. Hang the loin for 12 to 18 hours in a room that is between 70° and 80°F, with a high level of humidity—70 percent or so.

4. Move the loin to a cool, humid place and let it hang for 12 to 15 more days. If you see white mold, then it is a success. If you see green or black mold, wipe it off with a vinegar-soaked cloth. Now, cool and firm to the touch, it is ready to eat, though you can let it hang for longer if you wish. The longer it hangs, the dryer it becomes, but it's best when it's less dry. Wrap the *lonza* well and store it in the freezer to help it retain its moisture.

Note: Pink salt #2, is also known as Insta Cure #2, and Prague powder. It is a mixture of salt, sodium nitrate, and sodium nitrite, and used on meats that are dry cured over an extended period of time. The sodium nitrate breaks down over time to sodium nitrite, which then breaks down to nitric oxide, an oxidizing agent that keeps the meat safe from botulism. It can be bought from many places on the Internet, or you can ask your local butcher.

MAKES 1 PIG LOIN, CURED AND READY FOR A RAINY DAY

✹ GUANCIALE

Guanciale, dry-cured pork jowl, comes from the Italian word for cheek. The best way to use *guanciale* is to cut thick slices from it and then cut those slices into cubes. Render the fat from the cubes in a skillet and toss all of that with coarse dandelion greens or kale. Toss in other accoutrements that make you happy, such as pistachios and red onion slices. The sweetness from the *guanciale* and the acid from the dandelion marry well.

> Two pork jowls, 1 kilogram (2 pounds) each
> 140 grams (1 cup) kosher salt
> 140 grams (⅔ cup) sugar
> 5 grams (1 teaspoons) pink salt #1 (see Note page 37)
> 30 black peppercorns, coarsely ground, plus more for sprinkling
> 20 grams (½ tablespoon) fennel seeds, toasted and coarsely ground,
>   plus more for sprinkling
> 1 large bunch fresh thyme
> 6 allspice berries, coarsely ground (you can coarsely grind these and
>   peppercorns by pressing down on them with a pot or pan).

1. Remove the skin from the jowls. Then flip each one over to remove any glands and dried-out fat and meat. (Your butcher will do this for you if you ask.)
2. Combine all the remaining ingredients and mix well to make a cure. Place the jowls in a nonreactive container in which they fit snugly. Rub the cure all over the jowls, massaging thoroughly into the meat and fat. If you prefer, you can place them in a resealable bag.
3. Cure the jowls in the refrigerator, flipping them over once a day to make sure they cure evenly, for 7 to 10 days, until the jowls feel firm throughout.

4. Rinse the jowls well under cold water. Pat them dry, then sprinkle with additional cracked black pepper and toasted fennel seeds. Wrap in cheesecloth and hang to dry in a cool room, like the cellar, for another 1 to 3 weeks, depending on temperature and humidity, until completely stiff to the touch but not hard. Guanciale can be used immediately, or wrapped well and refrigerated for up to 3 weeks or frozen for up to 4 months.

MAKES 2 HANDSOME PORK JOWLS

JEAN-BENOÎT HUGUES

The Olive Farmer

CHAPTER SIX

Les Beaux, France

Healing with Olive Oil

I am spending the morning watching men strike oil—the kind that flows freely through the underbelly of Provence. The owner of this place, Jean-Benoît Hugues, is striding around in his quilted vest and threadbare jeans, with his floppy hair and furrowed brow, carefully inspecting machines and overseeing workers. White vans drive in and out of the gates like clockwork in time to machines stripping, spitting, washing, shredding, and spinning.

It began with a plot of land elevated along a slope in Les Beaux and a promise to an old man that they would never build on it. It was called Castelas, a field of four-hundred-year-old trees where a mystical combination of rock, sun, and age produces the best olive oil of all the subsequent forty-five hectares the Hugues' purchased. And so an oil earned its name, a hobby became a profession, and a husband and wife, Jean-Benoît and Catherine, improved their own execution of small-scale olive oil production and established a strong *terroir*—the taste of a place.

On this morning, there is a palpable solemnity in the light October air. Catherine is missing. Anticipating the harvest, I had been eagerly e-mailing her all fall like an impatient child in a long car ride asking, "Are we there yet?" Red crates of green olives are stacked sky-high against the backdrop of Les Beaux's round mountains. People are working diligently, but very quietly. And then I learn why. Catherine's father, one of the great owners of Châteauneuf-du-Pape, had died just hours earlier.

So, Jean-Benoît, pushing forward with the enormous task at hand, takes me under his wing—and up into the vast mountains of one of the most beautiful places in France. "It really was a healing thing," he says, fielding blind turns in his white truck. "See, I was in a high-tech business before. Stress, suit, tie, fast lane. I needed a change, and we started this as a hobby. And of course as you get into it you want to improve it. It's fun because this tree is very complex. You have to earn your marks with it; it's not given." Jean-Benoît has a history in America's Southwest oil province as well; he developed a strong appreciation for cultural identity working in Lubbock, Texas. He brought this spirit with him when he returned to Provence fifteen years later and, along with Catherine, turned it into an olive oil farm called Castelas.

As we wind up the mountains and the road becomes a black squiggle against the panoramic view, I see that the olive tree is truly a remarkable product of nature, and that France's olive trees are a particular reminder of this. In 1956 Provence lost all of its olive trees to frost. Demonstrating extraordinary endurance, the roots developed new trunks around the circumference of the old. Where there was once one, now there were five.

This in effect changed the future of French olive oil in that it could never be harvested in the same manner as the olive oil in Italy and Spain. The many-armed trunks would never cooperate with such technological advances in olive picking as the "trunk shaker"—a clamp surrounded by a large net that violently shakes the tree at the base and captures the olives. But even with the shaker, there is still a lot of handwork to be done. So with olives in general—and in France in particular—you must possess a singular devotion, early in the crisp mornings of late October, well into the even colder evenings of late November.

Out of the truck and onto the fields, workers move methodically tugging on the olives, milking the trees bare. They come over one by one, greeting me with their meaty handshakes and leathered faces. Traditionally, during the olive harvest, men and women from surrounding towns would arrive to perform the labor, doing what their parents and grandparents had done for generations. In the days when people were less mobile, the olive harvest was when members of isolated villages had an opportunity to meet each other—and often, form romantic attachments, high up in the olive trees. Though times have changed, the French olive-picking technique has not—it is still much the same as it was two millennia ago. The *bache*, a large plastic sheet, is placed around the base of the tree to catch the olives. A short-handled rake with blunt teeth is used to comb the olives from the lower branches. Then a picker uses a triangular ladder to climb to the top of the tree for the rest. Jean-Benoît's crew is sporting modern electric rakes powered by orange battery packs strapped to their backs. Now the electric rakes have extendable arms, and the days of ladders in France are gone. (Workmen's comp was too expensive and the rate of injury was too high.) Even so, the labor during harvest is still the most expensive part of the process. The family tradition of olive picking is tapering off, Jean-Benoît says. "Many of the pickers are old, and it is very hard to find pickers of the younger generations; they don't want to do it. So we have to adjust."

After all of the work that goes into picking olives, only about 20 percent of them end up as oil. The discards are pressed, and what remains is returned right back to the trees where they came from in the form of *prignon*, a natural olive fertilizer that looks like a bright green tapenade. Trucks drive by full of it on their way to pump it into a cylinder and shoot it out onto the fields. "We are almost fully organic," Jean-Benoît says, lighting a cigarette and pointing to the rows of prignon covering the field. "It is very difficult to control all of the weeds, so we are working on solutions. Ultimately—two, three years—we will be there." Then he makes a point to tell me that this is the only time of year he smokes.

———

A single liter of extra-virgin olive oil requires more than ten pounds of olives and dozens of steps that Jean-Benoît executes meticulously. Crates of olives are picked and processed within three hours to avoid "must," the fermentation that results from sitting. They are stripped of sticks and leaves, then washed in a tank of water. The varieties of olives are crushed separately, and the oil is extracted at below 27°C, about 80.6°F, to preserve its fresh flavor. Using a higher temperature would extract more oil, but sacrifice taste, so Jean-Benoît avoids it. As a result, his oil has a low acidity level that averages 0.15 grams per 100 grams of fat and a peroxide index of less than 7 milli equivalent per kilogram of fat—it's extra-virgin olive oil with a very long shelf life. There are two other levels of virginity in olive oil. If the free acid count is more than 1 but less than 1.5 you have *vierge fine*. More than 1.5 and up to 3.3 can only qualify as virgin—*vierge ordinaire*. Jean-Benoît does not produce these lesser grades.

After the crushing and pressing, the olives, now a green sludge, are whirled around in a centrifuge. The resulting lime-green liquid makes its way through a pipeline and pours out a spout into a pool, where the white foam, the remaining impurities, are skimmed from the surface. The oil then descends into tanks in the floor below. It was once thought that the pits should be painstakingly separated from the flesh to make high-quality olive oil, but it was then discovered that olive oil processed without pits went rancid quickly. Preservative properties in the pits make them integral to the process—just one more reminder not to mess with Mother Nature.

The oils of different olive varieties are kept separately in the underground tanks and mixed later to adhere to A.O.C., or *appellation d'origine controlée*, standards. Jean-Benoît can tell you the field where each olive comes from, much like wine. He produces four varieties of olives: Aglandau, Grossane, Salonenque, and Verdale.

France will never produce the same quantity of olive oil as Italy or Spain, so instead French olive oil makers compete on quality. And as with everything gastronomically great in France, that means it is controlled by committee. The A.O.C. is a third-party panel—a team of experts who monitor all things flavorful. Each product is tested, the producer and his methods scrutinized, and official forms completed. And of course, the A.O.C. inspectors get to eat their way from town to town in the name of maintaining quality. The rules are strict, regardless of the product: the appellation must come from a specified region, origin, and the quality must be of a particularly high standard. It is a system that protects culinary nuance, that savoir faire that makes it distinctly French. It also prevents impostors, and guarantees that consumers get the highest quality for their money.

Whereas with grapes, winemakers must be poised to pick at the pivotal moment, olives are forgiving. Jean-Benoît sends his olives to Aix, where he has a lab and a panel of tasters who convene and produce notes based on organoleptic parameters like intensity of smell, harmony of smell, softness, heat, harmony in the mouth, heaviness, bitterness, and body. But he also applies a more casual method. "I taste them. They tell me when they are no good," he says. The flavor of good olive oil is one of the oldest and purest, unchanged by centuries of innovation. The primitive, sinuous trunks, the spreading yawn of the branches, the metallic flicker of the silver-gray leaves give me a distinct sense that I am tasting and living time.

I stick my hands into a crate of olives and feel their pulpy leather skin against mine. Rather than the salty satisfaction of a table olive, there is the taste of black pepper, green leaves, unripe banana, papaya, black coffee—and model airplane glue. A finishing olive oil like Castelas should be strong and have a bite. Jean-Benoît describes each oil as he hands me spoonful after spoonful and they fall to the back of my mouth and lubricate my throat with pepper and pineapple. I experience the delayed but sometimes fierce scratching at the back of my head, then the delicate ones that rest on my tongue kindly like dessert. And later, I learn the ethereal taste of raw oil poured over hot food.

Jean-Benoît will make about 200,000 bottles this year—the biggest harvest he has ever had. And even with life now at a more manageable pace than it once was, he still has the impervious instincts of a businessman. "The question is how we are going to sell the oil," he says, now cruising through a valley between the hills around us. "I don't think we can increase the sales as much as we can increase the production. So we'll probably sell in bulk, which is never good financially. It's a very high-quality olive oil."

There is, though, a rising market for artisanal oils around the world, and he is beginning to receive orders from Cyprus, Germany, Saudi Arabia, and most surprisingly, the titans of olive oil, Italy and Spain.

The United States is also one of the largest importers. But as with any sudden fad, it presents a particular dilemma. He fields a deluge of calls from his truck, French rolling off his tongue in double-time. Finally hanging up, he says, smiling, "That's a copycat. I don't like copycats." His neighbor at a nearby estate has sold his biscuit factory to Dannon and has taken up olive oil production as a hobby. Jean-Benoît worries about the shortcuts his neighbor is taking because it dilutes the artisanal standard that is already under threat.

"If you cannot claim the artisanal way of doing things then you cannot pay for it," he says. "People need something to hang on to if they're going to pay the higher cost. There is something extra in it, there is the culture. You're buying a piece of an area, you're buying a piece of culture. It's a bit of a luxury. Luxury is not a bad word. I really believe in that more and more, it's part of our diet. It doesn't mean you can't improve it and you can't use technology. And I'm a good example of that. But at the same time you have to retain what's essential—the land, the way of living, the varieties, the taste. If you don't take those steps then nothing sets you apart." He says the diluted reputation of Chardonnay wine is an example of what can happen to olive oil if it is not protected. "I remember buying Chardonnay from Chateau Sainte Michelle in Washington state. If you're too close to a grape, you forget the name of the winery, you forget the people behind it, the name of the area where it comes from. You forget the hands of the man and woman. These values as you get older become more and more important. And I think young people are starting to care also."

In America, a handful of cowboys in Lubbock, Texas, taught Jean-Benoît that simple passions, like the passion for barbecue sauce, can reflect a strong cultural identity. He is a barbecue fanatic. "I like it if it's peppery, made with good honey, and smoky, with a good rib, a hand full of it. In English, you use the phrase 'the sense of belonging.' It's important because people don't usually belong to many places. In Lubbock, Texas, people belonged there. I take pride in reflecting a sense of place in my olive oil."

Entering the front gates of the mill and parking the van under trees flush with terra-cotta-colored persimmons, I begin to see how this is all a little curative. Splitting open a persimmon, I walk up the moss-laced stone steps to the tasting room. There my nostrils open to the ripe, bright smell of pressing olives. The hum of the machines is comforting. Jean-Benoît is about to pour me the very first bottle of the season. I put down the persimmon, and there form my own romantic attachment to olive oil. "Oil is like a child," he explains, removing a forest-green bottle from a case. "Here you have the perfect demonstration of that." He attaches the spout to the bottle and slowly fills it. "You taste it and it's very difficult to grasp. And then in December, January, it's going to slow down and it's going to be more of a teenager, still a little moody." He presses a cork into the mouth of the bottle, covers it with a metal wrapper, and seals it with heat. "Then in February it's going to be long and calm." He presses a label onto the bottle and hands it to me.

It is true that this is more than just a hobby by now for Jean-Benoît and Catherine. But they have a vision that motivates them not to expand beyond the confines of their artisan standards. "We will not exceed the size of the mill. We want to keep our soul, a way of sharing our passion . . . it's a healing thing," he reminds me. Then with a quick salute, he makes his way back through the gates toward the humming machines.

Driving away from Castelas, I rock sideways to the current of the autumn mistral winds and to French country music. I could easily be in Lubbock, listening to similar music, riding past similar hills. Jean-Benoît's zeal for olive oil and barbecue is a reflection of the same thing—pursuit of identity, sense of place, and excellence. This is the way he is leaving his mark.

✒ HOW TO TASTE OLIVE OIL

There is something romantic about good olive oil, and also noble. Olives can endure more abuse than grapes, and the oil has healing powers when consumed by the spoonful or when applied to the skin. And unlike most wines, it is always best used while young, in the first year. Even the best olive oils, when stored properly, don't last beyond a few years.

Peppery, bitter, and green are all words you will hear to describe good olive oil, but probably not for good wine. The method of tasting oil and wine, though, is very much the same.

1. Tear off a piece of bread from a warm, crusty loaf. The heat from the loaf will take the olive oil just above room temperature, which is ideal for tasting.
2. Push your thumbs into the soft center of the bread to make an indent.
3. Fill the indent with olive oil. The color can be many shades of yellow and green, but it should not be clear, which indicates that it didn't come from the first pressing.
4. Get your nose in there and breathe in deeply. "Take in the bouquet," as they say. Breathe until you can taste it.
5. Take small sips, tilt your head back, and swish the oil to your back teeth.
6. Take in a few deep breaths to suck in the air and gather all those organoleptic traits. And swallow.
7. Eat the bread and lick your thumbs. Wipe your greasy chin.

OLIVE OIL MUFFINS

The amount of olive oil in these muffins gives them a crusty top and moist middle. They can be considered savory or sweet by themselves but they also pair well with things like goat cheese, sun-dried tomatoes, marmalade, or lemon curd. And the smell of the kitchen as they cook is unforgettable.

> 1 cup all-purpose flour
> 1 cup almond flour
> 1 ½ cups powdered sugar
> 1 teaspoon salt
> 8 large egg whites
> 1 cup olive oil

1. Preheat the oven to 400°F.
2. Grease a standard muffin pan.
3. In a large, heavy bowl (one that you can whisk in without holding on to it), combine all of the dry ingredients. Then, with a whisk, slowly stir in the egg whites until they are fully incorporated; be sure to whisk gently so that you don't incorporate too much air. Then, in a slow, thin, steady stream, pour in the oil with one hand while whisking with the other, making sure the oil is fully incorporated before continuing the stream, and not letting any pools form. Refrigerate the batter for 15 minutes. Stir briefly.
4. Fill the muffin cups three-quarters full of batter; the muffins will rise quite a bit.
5. Bake for 15 minutes, then lower the oven temperature to 350°F and bake for 15 minutes more, or until the muffins are golden brown on top.

MAKES 12 OLIVE OIL MUFFINS

✒ MAUREEN'S PESTO

In the Hudson Valley where I grew up, there is a woman named Maureen. She happens to make world-renowned pesto. She also happens to be my mother. In far-reaching corners of the earth people try to emulate its greatness, and fail. This is her recipe. The secret lies in copious garlic and coarsely chopped walnuts.

If you are lucky, and have a lot of extra basil, blend it well without adding anything but olive oil. Then freeze it; later, thaw it and add the remaining ingredients.

2 tightly packed cups fresh basil leaves
½ cup olive oil, or more as needed
8 cloves garlic
½ teaspoon salt
1 teaspoon black pepper
¾ cup walnuts
½ cup grated Parmesan cheese

1. In a food processor, combine the basil, oil, garlic, salt, and pepper until well blended.
2. Add the walnuts and cheese and pulse 10 times for a chunky consistency.
3. Taste and adjust to your liking.

MAKES 2 CUPS OF GREATNESS

UNLIKELY WAYS TO USE OLIVE OIL

1. Olive oil mixed with rosemary soothes sore, stiff muscles. Heated, this mixture serves as a scalp-stimulating deep hair conditioner when left in for 15 minutes.
2. Olive oil on a cotton swab serves as an eye-makeup remover.
3. Olive oil and mint applied to the temples is said to cure migraines.
4. A tablespoon of olive oil taken before a large feast will lubricate the stomach lining, and soften a hangover. It will also stimulate digestion and relieve an upset stomach.
5. A few drops in a bubble bath soothes and softens the skin, as does applying it to the face or cuticles at night.
6. Because of its lovely traits, it is said that a daily dose of olive oil will help you live longer.

BILL BEST

The Seed Librarian

CHAPTER SEVEN

Berea, Kentucky

The Seed Saver

With a cardboard box of twine strapped to his waist, Bill wraps his hand around a golden Vinson Watts tomato and walks the high tunnels of his hoop barn in pinstriped overalls. Red, yellow, orange, green, black, and purple tomatoes color the canvas floor in a dotted line.

He speaks at a quiet tempo, barely audible above the greenhouse fan. "One of my friends worked on that one for fifty-two years," he says, holding the Vinson Watts. "It's my best-selling tomato." He pulls twine from his belt to secure the tops of the tomato plants to their poles, his thin white hair iridescent in the muted greenhouse light, his face lined from years of squinting into the Kentucky sun. "See, none of these would be USDA number one. That's a serious problem for the consumer because most Americans living today have no idea what a good tomato is. They just simply don't. I don't have anything against hybrids—this is one is a hybrid—but I have something against the modern plant breeders claiming that hybrids are more disease resistant than heirlooms, because that's simply not true. That's how an heirloom became an heirloom: because it was worth saving. You don't save a seed that's disease prone; you simply don't do that." He goes and collects the last ones for the farmers' market later that afternoon.

Bill Best specializes in heirloom beans and tomatoes in Berea, Kentucky, but has been planting vegetables almost all his life—since he was two years old and Grandpa Best began teaching him the differences between young sweet potato and cocklebur. As a child raised in the mountains of North Carolina, he spent his days with his mother in the gardens of their home. Each summer Bill helped her pick wild nuts and berries, which they depended on. He became an expert, and climbed all over the mountains to pick the finest wild blackberries. Mother Best was eager to learn new things, but she also believed strongly in preserving the best of the old. Each summer Bill helped her pick the various cornfield beans to be eaten fresh, canned, or saved as seed for the following year's crop.

But it wasn't until one Christmas, thirty years later, that Bill fully realized that Mother Best was far ahead of her time. She had intuitively felt that the new beans offered by the seed companies, and the old beans that had been "improved" by plant breeders, were lacking. She noticed they were increasingly bland and tough and had none of the flavor and tenderness of the beans that had been passed down in the mountains for generations. Every fall, when Bill visited his family as a young man, Mother Best gave him dried beans she had saved and reminded him that he ought to be growing them and not the ones he was buying from the big suppliers. Eventually he listened and then began to realize that the natural and rapid mutation of the bean had led to a fascinating cultural and culinary phenomenon in the South. Families were passing on beans with their family's name, claiming they were the best to be found. The bean strains were passed on from generation to generation, migrating as daughters married sons from other bean stock and, in turn, their beans not only "married" but, in different sunlight and soil, mutated into a new bean.

Bill began to see that this rich diversity of heirloom beans was being lost to the commercial production of homogenous hybrid strains bred for hardiness and disease resistance—but never taste or character. It only took a simple observation—noticing how bad the flavor was in the seeds he bought from seed catalogs, that they produced food with less taste than that of his youth, that the texture was tougher. At first it didn't occur to him that the seeds he bought at the farm stores might be genetically altered for purposes other than making them more nutritious and tasty. But then he realized that something bad was happening. Vegetables were being grown to accommodate machinery, to be machine picked. And he thought that was terrible, because the flavor and texture—and nutrition—were being removed in the process.

And so he began the Sustainable Mountain Agriculture Center (SMAC) in Berea, Kentucky, setting out to preserve traditional seed stock. Soon he was asking people to send him the stories that went along with their beans—how they got their names, whose family or community they came from—and he committed these stories to heart. And then one day, the world began to see the value in what he was doing. Having been hopelessly behind the times for decades, he was suddenly en vogue. Soon hundreds and then thousands of people wanted to participate in the seed program. He lets them, though he does sometimes wonder if some people really get it. "You get so many volunteers who come out of some sort of upper-middle-class guilt, to share their riches without realizing that they have not yet acquired any riches. For me this project is not just romantic; it makes sense."

Bill Best's farm is set on a narrow road against a mountain. Berea is surrounded by mountains with names like Button Lick Knob, Wolf Gap, and Dead Horse. Most of the family, from his son to his great-grandson, live on the farm in various houses that freckle the land. The smell of his wood-burning stove drifts through the woods to greet visitors. He gets the wood off the mountain—he goes and collects it himself—to heat the greenhouses, which he tries to keep at a stable temperature because tomatoes ripen faster when they have a steady temperature between 70° and 75°F.

When he first started selling produce in 1972, he was the youngest member of the Lexington, Kentucky, farmers' market; now he is the oldest. He also frequents the Berea market, which he started himself in 1973 by getting his neighbors to begin selling their goods. Down in the town, he is known as the "master tomato guy." For thirty-four years he ran the Berea market himself, and there, too, he started out as the youngest farmer and now is the oldest.

He lines his tomatoes neatly in a crate and says, "I used to be considered just way behind the times. And I got so far behind the times that eventually when the curve reversed I was ahead of it. It worked out well for me. But it was certainly nothing planned."

Farmers' markets and restaurants are where most of his tomatoes end up these days. He tried selling to the commercial market many years before, but his first experience wasn't good. "I took some ripe tomatoes to a produce house in Lexington where they had several big stores they delivered to, and I asked them if they'd be interested in me bringing them tomatoes. And a man down there he tasted one and said, 'Yes, this is an excellent tomato. I'll take all you have.'" So Bill, his young children, and wife picked the first ripe clusters of tomatoes, took photos of them because they looked so good, loaded them in the station wagon, and brought them to the produce house.

"He seemed to think I was stupid because I wasn't aware of the standard way of marketing tomatoes in grocery stores," Bill says. "The buyer got very upset. He said, 'You brought me ripe tomatoes. I want green tomatoes. I'll keep them in storage and when one of my stores wants tomatoes I'll load them in the truck and gas them on the way, and by the time they get there they'll be red.' So I pretty well walked out on him. He was very upset and he made me upset, too. He said, 'You're ignorant,' and I said, 'Yes, I am, if you want green tomatoes that you're going to gas.' So that was the only time I had an experience like that. Since that time forward I have not fooled with places that use ethylene gas. It turns them sickly pink. I think it gives them a very bad taste. They never totally ripen."

This was an astounding revelation to Bill that changed his work and motivated him further. He began to notice that those tomatoes that win the national prizes as "All Americans" were not necessarily the best—or even good at all. He began to realize that even tomatoes were affected by politics.

He selects a few tomatoes for lunch, and we walk up the gravel road to the farmhouse. For a few minutes, we make mayonnaise and tomato sandwiches in silence, spreading a healthy layer of mayonnaise over white bread, putting on layers of tomato thicker than the bread itself. With each bite, my fingers press through the bread and dissolve into the tomato.

"When I was a child, I used to take them with me as my lunch, as long as we had tomatoes," he tells me around a little laminate table in his living room. "Then when we ran out of large tomatoes I'd pack the little Tommie Toes and put them on. Then when we ran out of tomatoes altogether I'd take mayonnaise sandwiches for about two weeks and pretend I was eating tomato sandwiches. I've always loved tomatoes. It's my favorite food."

His most memorable year as a child was when there wasn't frost until after Thanksgiving and he could pick ripe tomatoes for Thanksgiving dinner. "Such was, and continues to be, my love of tomatoes," he says, making another sandwich.

He passes me a platter of sliced ones and gives me a taste test. The Momotaro, translated to "Tough Boy," is one of his best sellers. Japanese women in Lexington fill their bags when they spot them. The color is pink, the skin is crisp. It is higher in acid than the Vinson Watts, his personal favorite. He has me try different layers of the Vinson Watts, the inside slices are sweeter than the outside. Fleshy and meaty, it is like cutting into a dessert. Bill says, "Tomorrow at the Lexington market when I put these out, they will last about fifteen minutes."

There is a visceral appeal to a pile of pink, brown, black, orange, purple, white, green, and striped tomatoes with all different shapes—oblong, flat with ribs, heart shaped, ruffled, or even shaped like peppers. And they possess such jolly names like Lemon Boy, Golden Boy, Yellow German, Pineapple, Big Rainbow, Georgia Streak, Hillbilly, Kentucky Beefsteak, Boyd Smith, Willard Wynn, Zeke Dishman, and Anna Russian. All offer variations on a common flavor, with thirty flavor components that dance the acid-sugar tango, and change as the season progresses.

Why have so many plant breeders tried to make tomatoes rounder and rounder, and more uniform in shape, while others still have tried to make them square so that they will fit into boxes more easily? Bill thinks this is the reason why a lot of people don't like tomatoes these days, at least not like they used to. "It's the way they're developed," he says, "the way they're grown, the way they're packaged, the way they're transported, the way they're gassed and colored later. They're never given a chance to become ripe." He finds himself selling to a lot of mothers who want their children to learn to like tomatoes.

In April he bought a tomato from a megamart to test it, then waited and waited for it to ripen. "After we finally cut it to eat it, it smelled of formaldehyde and had a really bad taste. So I decided we won't waste it, we'll feed it to the chickens. Normally if we feed them tomato scraps from our tomatoes they rush over and eat them as fast as they can. Well, these chickens rushed over and then ran away as fast as they could. That's a true story. The chickens ran away. And two weeks later, those tomato slices were still laying there on the ground. They had not begun to deteriorate at all. I think there's a real story there: they're indestructible."

This year, Bill is growing fifty to sixty varieties of heirloom tomatoes; he used to grow 150. He is still doing a lot of experimenting. And though he doesn't grow nearly as many varieties as he used to, he grows more total plants. What he has found is that the ones from this area, from southern Appalachia, are in particularly good shape because the soil is ideal in this part of the country.

He is also growing sixty varieties of beans this year, and has collected 440 varieties of beans from the region. He sells his tomato and bean seeds by mail order in the United States and Canada.

"I'm known more for my beans than for my tomatoes in the academic world," he says, "but in the food world, I'm known for my tomatoes." People are sending him seeds all the time. He has received forty-plus varieties just since he had his seed savers meeting in the barn six months ago in October. They arrive from all over the country, from people once from Appalachia, who have moved and maintained their family beans—people who have never met him.

In the shed, he has two freezers full of seeds. "Here are the beans that I'm resurrecting from oblivion," he says, wading through frozen bags containing more than 420 bean varieties. He lifts one small package from a box containing a few anonymous seeds. "A lady sent me a hundred of these that she couldn't germinate. There are now about ten beans between these and extinction and I'm going to germinate them one by one. It's called the Noble bean."

He pulls out his own family bean, the kind that Mother Best used to can, then a few packages of red-and-white-speckled Trail of Tears, then Shelley Beans, the kind you shell while they're still wet so they don't have to be rehydrated, then one called Red Ribbon. He explains that the Greasy bean has a slick hull, almost like it has been dipped in oil. It is considered to be one of the best-tasting beans. "Well, you know about cars," he says, "the Blue Lake is the Yugo of beans, the Greasy bean is the Maserati. There's that much difference. There truly is."

It all began when he invited people who came to the farmers' market in Lexington to bring him samples of seeds they talked about, and they did. His seed collection includes arrivals from twenty years ago. He sometimes gets photographs from people who are close to one hundred years old and are still saving their seeds. Sometimes they bring seeds from a freezer that belonged to a grandparent who had been dead for a decade. Each seed has its own story and its own name, often that of the person who propagated it first. Before they saved them in their freezers, they kept them among mothballs, and before that they stored them with hot peppers. Bean seeds are remarkably durable; seeds found in the pyramids of South America have been germinated after five thousand years.

"We have Cut Short beans that have been grown from fourteen hundred years ago. So we know certain beans have been here for a long time. The largest variety of beans is in this part of the country. It took other people to make me recognize that I had treasure in my hands. Once lost, these plants will never be available again. My granddaughter is a fifth-generation seed saver, I'm a third-generation seed saver. Of course, when you go back further than that, most everyone was a seed saver—they had to be. It started with the Indians."

An earlier crop is the best way to make sure you preserve old varieties. But this year's bean crop is just beginning to fill in, because the weather has been especially wet. In the fields the vines dangle on white threads. Bill has developed his own special way of tying them up as they grow. It is an intricate looming process that he likens to a kind of meditation.

After showing me the contents of his freezers, and with a belly full of tomato sandwiches, Bill lies back in his reclining chair and completely conks out. In under thirty seconds, he descends into a deep afternoon sleep.

When he resurfaces, we put our boots back on and go down to the blueberry patches. We position two plastic chairs side by side and begin to pull handfuls of berries into containers. This too has a meditative current to it. As the hot sun beats down on us, the tart blueberries make my mouth water for more. And as Bill talks in his quiet cadence, I strain to listen, for I have learned by now that if I don't I will miss real wisdom.

Though he has a doctorate in Appalachian studies, he tells me that his theoretical specialty is aesthetics, which he says has to do with harmonizing thinking and feeling—a blend of the arts and conceptual thinking. He also has a master's degree in . . . modern dance. "I've been all around the block," he says to me. "I've not wholly specialized in anything. I did most of my real work in terms of choreography in aquatic arts. I prefer that because you have many different levels you can work from with a diving board. Dance is a little bit too inhibiting because of gravity. But I enjoy working with the arts. I enjoyed the freedom of modern dance and the way it made you discipline yourself. I also did a little bit of ballet." Dance was always an important part of life in his home community.

"I've found that it's better to be yourself than an imitation of someone else," he says. "I've never said in so many years that I wanted to be such and such. I took a bunch of tests in college. Preference inventories and things like that. And they kept calling me back to retake them. And so I kept going back and faithfully retaking them, and finally they said, 'Well, according to this test, you don't know what you want to do.' And I said, 'Well, you know, I could have told you that without taking any kind of test at all. I'm interested in everything.' And so that's the last time they called me to take the exam. I was naïve, but then I thought, well, that's what life is all about."

Bill's expertise in heirloom seeds stems from this keen interest in everything. SMAC formed simply because nobody had any interest in taking over his seed collection and for him the logical answer was to create a not-for-profit organization with his son and a few friends to save these valuable seeds—they are valuable in their heritage, which to him is equal to any other kind of value. For a long time they weren't having much luck getting grants, and were struggling to break even. The agricultural departments at colleges weren't interested in sustainable agriculture.

"Whenever the University of Kentucky has a need for something on heirlooms they have people contact me," he says soberly. "It should be the reverse: I should be referring people to them instead of them referring people to me. But see, they get most of their grant money from the feed, seed, food, and chemical companies. They don't get any research money from people doing what I'm doing. I guess they have to feed the mouth that bites them." He laughs, pauses for a while to pick more blueberries, then says, "I still have to write a modern-day version of 'Jack and the Beanstalk' where I'm going to have the Giant win only temporarily because there's enough people like me who will be the Jacks of the world out there fighting them."

Twenty-nine packages of blueberries later, Bill has taught me well. We climb into his truck with the day's harvest and drive down the narrow wooded road to the farmers' market, the same road he has traveled for thirty-four years. He tells me about his life, and how precious his traditions are to him. How personal they can become. "I grew up with very little money. My parents were truly subsistence farmers. But I thought we had the most wonderful diet on earth. And time has proven me correct on that. We raised all of our own food. We did have the best diet. We even took our wheat to be ground into flour and our corn to be ground into cornmeal. For Americans today, everything is anonymous when it comes to food."

He continues, "Everything was done by barter. We would take the corn and wheat and leave part of it to pay for the grinding, so very little money ever changed hands. My father would go into town and trade his eggs for coffee and sugar or molasses. My mother was an early riser, getting up to go out to awaken the roosters so that they might go out and crow to awaken everyone else. She made hominy and cottage cheese from scratch. She would make her hominy by using the lye from wood ashes. Everything we did, we did by hand. We never went shopping at the supermarket. I never heard that word until I went to college."

We back the truck up to the small town square in front of Berea College and set up the farm stand. Bill has it down to a science. All of the customers come to hang out and watch us set up. People are already lining up for the tomatoes and blueberries before the table is set down before them. By the time the truck door is closed, people are piling red, yellow, and orange tomatoes onto the scale.

"I'm not doing anything really differently than what I've always done; I'm just doing more of it," he says simply. Like his mother, Bill has become one of those universal people. He understands Appalachian culture in a profound and complex way, and he has devoted much of his life to teaching others about it. He has been saving beans and tales for years, planting small crops to build up specific seed stock. He has done the same for his other favorite food, tomatoes. After years of seed saving, the ground Bill walks is green with beanstalks and tomato plants. He has become a bit of an heirloom treasure himself.

✹ BEANS AND CURED FATBACK OR JUST GOOD BACON

In the Upper Crabtree community in Haywood County, North Carolina, in the 1940s and 1950s, Bill Best grew up on pork. His mother canned hams and sold the ones that they cured, for a cured ham would bring as much as a whole hog on the market. Mother Best was also an early riser, who before sunrise set about making delicious things with the ingredients at hand.

If you have time, it is helpful to soak your dried beans for 24 hours before you cook them so they cook a little more quickly; soaking will also help them cook more uniformly. This recipe is easily adapted, and will take on any other vegetables and seasonings you add to it.

1 tablespoon olive oil
1 medium onion, diced
¾ pound cured fatback, or 4 slices bacon, diced
2 bay leaves
3 cloves garlic, crushed
2 cups dried beans
1 teaspoon red wine vinegar
2 teaspoons salt
Black pepper to taste

1. Heat the oil in a large saucepan over medium heat. Add the onion and fatback and cook until the onion is soft. Add the bay leaves and garlic and cook until the garlic is soft. Add the beans and stir them for a few minutes to "blanch" the skins. Cover them with water by about 2 inches (about 8 cups) and add the salt and pepper.
2. Simmer, covered, over low heat for 2½ hours, until tender.
3. Add the vinegar and more salt and pepper to taste. Mother Best served them with white cornbread.

MAKES 6 CUPS BEANS

✤ CANNED TOMATOES

Bill's wife freezes and cans leftover tomato juice. She also quarters tomatoes and freezes them in resealable plastic bags. My father and I have always canned tomatoes for the winter and put them on the mantle to admire, and we'd open them one by one during the coldest months. They are a spectacular treat in February when the taste of August's tomatoes is a thin memory.

Ripe tomatoes, plum or otherwise
Salt
Fresh basil, dried bay leaves, or other herbs (optional)

1. Bring a large pot of water to a boil and prepare another large bowl of ice water. Wash the tomatoes. With the tip of a paring knife, cut around the core at the top of the tomato and pop it out.
2. Drop the tomatoes into the boiling water for 30 seconds, or until the skins begin to crack. Remove them with a slotted spoon and drop them quickly into the cold water. Slip off the tomato skins.
3. Leave them whole or cut them into quarters or halves. Pack them in clean glass canning jars, pressing down gently after each two tomatoes are added to release juice and fill the spaces. Add an herb leaf or sprig to each jar, if you'd like. Leave ½ inch headspace at the top.
4. Place the flat lids and screw bands on top and tighten them gently. Submerge the jars in boiling water for 45 minutes. Remove them from the water. You will hear a fun "popping" sound as they cool, which indicates that they are sealing. At this point you can tighten the lids.

MAKES MANY JARS OF AUGUST MEMORIES

⚼ HOW TO BE AN HEIRLOOM SEED SAVER

1. Keep an eye out for mutations. That is how "family beans" start; one bean mutates from a particular variety and, when replanted, stays true to its new form. Give it a name and call it your own.

2. Protect your seeds from becoming contaminated by commercial seeds containing the gene for toughness. If you must grow commercial seeds, put them far away from your heirlooms to avoid crossing, or plant them at different times so the flowers don't pollinate each other. This is especially true where there are a lot of bumblebees, which are aggressive with certain blossoms, including the bean blossom.

3. Don't plant all of your seeds of a particular variety. Instead, save a few in case they don't germinate or poor weather causes crop failure. This way you will never lose a variety completely.

4. Save the seeds that look most true to their form. Plant them again the following year to see if they stay true to type. If you plant your first seeds early enough, you can gain a season by planting a second crop from the freshly picked seeds.

5. Share your heirloom seeds with other growers to help keep them in circulation.

HANS-OTTO JOHNSEN

The Bee Savior

CHAPTER EIGHT

Skjeberg, Norway

Hans and the
50,000,000 Sisters

"I couldn't resist visiting bees on the way up," Hans-Otto Johnsen says, exhaling with a heavy Nordic laugh. He lifts the back of his navy Hyundai van—he calls it his "Korean tin can"—and slips my suitcase between stacks of beehive frames. The smell of beeswax drifts out into the airport parking lot, and we embark on a narrow journey of curved roads sandwiched between dense pencil firs, and he tells me tales of vinegar and honey.

Southern Norway is a land of moose and elk and reindeer—and dandelions frothing with pollen. It is where rolling green hills abut oceans of pine trees without transition. The simplicity of the barns and houses is satisfying to behold, built with a pleasing adherence to the golden mean. The landscape is dominated by red, green, and white. Contented horses rolling in the mud and a strange glut of vintage American automobiles—red 1957 Ford Fairlane convertibles—give the distinct impression you're living in a place where 1950s America meets a modern Amish landscape.

"I like bees, but I don't like flies!" Hans-Otto says, clapping the air, emitting another robust laugh. We chug along in his tin can, leaving a trail of beeswax fumes in our wake. But this journey really began on a day many years ago as Hans-Otto transported two tons of dynamite into a mine.

He had spent twenty years of his life as an industrial mechanic managing heavy factory equipment. On that fateful day, though, nitroglycerine from the dynamite permeated his skin, increased his heartbeat, and made him very sick. As he recovered, Hans-Otto's friend, who had beehives, asked him to help move the bees during pollination season. And so began Hans-Otto's bond with bees, an unlikely occurrence that may have been providence.

"I want to make honey that is as pure as possible without all the pesticides," he says, lurching into an impassioned speech. To do that, he uses a method he calls "biological optimization": he rejects pesticides and acids when tending to his bees and instead uses selective breeding and a strict management system to help them fight predators.

He is working to save one of the most highly organized and complex societies in the animal world, one that is responsible for pollinating a large portion of the world's food source and has been mysteriously vanishing in an epidemic named "colony collapse disorder."

After driving for several hours we stop in the wooded outskirts of an apple orchard, step into white jumpsuits that look like hazmat suits, and fasten netted hoods to our heads. Hans-Otto begins to puff bellows of smoke around us, and I hear the bees become drowsy as the sound of their buzz hushes.

Beneath the frames, the beehive's internal structure is a densely packed matrix of honeycomb, the hexagonal cells brimming with food (honey and pollen) and brood (eggs, larvae, and pupae). The three-caste system is at work, the queen laying eggs in their rightful cells, the male drones loitering and waiting to be fed, the female workers busying themselves to death in thirty days or fewer.

The worker bees dance about my netted head, a special dance, the distance and direction of the pollen encoded symbolically in their moves. One lands on my net, looks me in the eye, then flies away—up to three miles away—to find pollen.

Her sisters delegate responsibility here in the woods, in their white-towered homes, amid the tall firs and the short pebbled grass.

They work quickly in their roles as cell-cleaning bees, nurse bees, wax-production bees, honey-capping bees, drone-feeding bees, queen attendants, pollen packers, mortuary bees, fanning bees, guard bees, water carriers, and foraging bees.

Hans-Otto lifts another frame and we look one layer farther into the hive, where I see a worker bee hatch, slowly eating her way out of a wax cocoon, struggling to set herself free as the others help her, soon succeeding, learning her purpose, and beginning her work.

No one knows for certain why bees around the world are struggling now. But Hans-Otto believes he has the key to a solution. He pulls out a map from his collection of old honey books that he keeps in a secret hiding place. The map shows where honeybees have been transported over time—from Europe to Asia, from North America to South America. He works particularly to combat the Varroa mite, a parasite that attaches to the body of the bee and sucks the life from it. He leafs through the brittle pages of his book and traces the bees' path—their journey first to Asia in a haystack aboard a ship, then to Germany with Professor Friedrich Ruttner, an Austrian-born scientist.

Even though the bees had been in Asia, homeland of the Varroa, for quite some time, they didn't begin to die from Varroa until Ruttner brought them to Germany. The difference was in the size of their wax cells. "They were transported to Asia in natural hives. The bees didn't crash immediately because they had their natural environment in the hay," says Hans-Otto. It wasn't until humans decided to increase the cell size of the hive frames from 4.92 to 5.3 millimeters for worker bees, and from 6.2 to 7.0 millimeters for drones, that the bees became unable to defend themselves against Varroa. Scientists believed that by increasing the cell size of the hives, the bees would produce more honey, because their bodies would become enlarged. But the bees never did produce more honey, they just became fluffy—obese—and vulnerable. Instead there were bees who, in some cases, were simply too big for their wings, a loud whirring buzz emanating from their bodies as they struggled to carry themselves along. Most beekeepers still use these large-cell frames today. But Hans-Otto doesn't. He uses natural cell sizes, and since he can't find anyone who will make them properly, he makes them himself.

"My approach to the mite problem is to reduce cell size to 4.92 millimeters. Bees have stayed the same for roughly fifteen million years; there hasn't been much evolution. When it hasn't changed over ten, fifteen million years, something's going right. So you adapt to their original habits." His bees look just like the bees in his ancient books—small and healthy.

And they groom themselves and fight the Varroa mite superbly, opening the cell tops of developing pupae prematurely when they detect mites in the cells, then eliminating the pupae that are infected with savage speed. When he has a hive that fends for itself in an accurate way, he isolates these bees and breeds them for their good genetics. He roams the woods, watching, observing, slipping a sheet of paper under a hive and examining what falls. "When I see light-colored mites and damaged mites, I know the bees are dealing with mites on their own—it's that simple."

In the summers, he selects thirty hives, ones that have survived well for several seasons and produced high honey volume. He lets his queens mate in this environment, in an isolated area dominated by good bees. He prefers this to relying on one queen repeatedly because it avoids inbreeding and immunodeficiency. His breeds are hearty. One called Buckfast was developed by a monk in England named Brother Adam, the other a Swedish breed called Elgon.

Hans-Otto's workshop is set back deep into the countryside of Skjeberg, in very southeast Norway, only miles from Sweden. Thirty minutes away is Halden, his birthplace, marked by three-hundred-year-old houses and a stone fortress set high upon a hill. On the way to his workshop we stop to visit his farmer friends, one who sells organic eggs at his front door and keeps a rare breed of workhorses that are nearly extinct; another who is an apple farmer and is expert at getting small trees to produce a lot of fruit.

We arrive at Hans-Otto's white clapboard home, and he is suddenly self-conscious of its appearance. It smacks of a place where many intricate experiments are being conducted, where things are happening. Stacks of unused hives are piled in the gravel driveway next to the peeling red barn that serves as his workshop. Hans-Otto cracks a raw egg and lets it fall to a paper plate on the ground. The cat scurries forward to consume it. Then we enter the barn.

It is like the laboratory kitchen of *Chitty Chitty Bang Bang*—rolls of flattened wax sheets piled high in a corner, scraps of wax shavings cast about in various heaps. Vats of wax stand side by side waiting to be heated and pushed through the pipes on their way to becoming precisely molded bee homes.

Hans-Otto is the only person in Norway, perhaps in Europe, capable of producing these bee homes. He spent six years perfecting them, and went to Kansas and Ohio to buy machines that he then tweaked, customized, and sometimes disassembled and rebuilt with parts he gathered from around the world. Other producers distort their wax foundations during the milling, centering, and embossing. This won't do for Hans-Otto. He rolls out thin sheets of wax of uniform thickness, then embosses them with the natural hexagonal cell shape upon which bees build their hives once the sheets are installed in frames. "When you are making beeswax into sheets it's difficult to avoid stretching. So I have worked very hard to come up with a quality control system so I don't get this stretching." When he is talking about a difference of less than 0.4 millimeters between healthy bees (4.92-millimeter cells) and unhealthy ones (5.3-millimeter cells), he cannot afford stretching from poor manufacturing.

He gazes around the room, the dusty light reflecting off his metal tools. "That roller is from Kansas, the motor is from China, those gears are from Germany, and those are complex driver frequency controllers from America. I made this equipment because it was impossible to buy exactly what I wanted. I am a very stubborn person." He turns it on and we listen to the humming and the squeaking.

He melts eleven hundred pounds of used wax in a double-jacketed tank and heats it to 120°C to kill all bacteria. He flushes impurities with water and strains the wax to remove wood and debris. He doesn't use bleach or clay to purify the wax the way many commercial producers do, because the residue it leaves will affect his bees. The system is entirely organic in the way he controls quality.

The wax pumps into a new tank, where it is converted into sheets as it mixes with cold water onto a spinning drum and hardens. Soon Hans-Otto has rolls of wax sheets that are 1.4 millimeters thick—thin compared to the standard 3.4-millimeter sheets typically produced.

With a small measuring device he demonstrates how perfectly even they are, how he has controlled such a malleable substance as wax and avoided stretching.

"I have spent six years testing, testing, testing, testing. The only option in Europe is the German machine. The stretching on that machine is tremendous. Up to 0.6 millimeters sometimes, which from my point of view is totally useless. There was no one in Europe that produced beeswax foundations naturally as I wanted it—without stretching, no bleaching; proper methods of killing bacteria. I didn't have a choice but to make it myself; the product was not available."

He pushes his wax sheets through embossing rollers made of soft metal, a combination of elements he asks me to keep secret, while a blade on the side cuts them to perfect width. He wets the machine so the beeswax doesn't stick to the warm parts. He holds up a 5.3-millimeter cell sheet against the light, then the 4.92-millimeter. "You can see with your bare eye that there is a difference," he says. Measuring with his tool again, his mind wanders elsewhere, as I inspect the minute, amazing difference between healthy and unhealthy bees.

Here Hans-Otto has found a perfect symbiosis between his former job and his new one—using his skills as an engineer to help the honey-bees. "Without my years with the process control, I would probably lose my money if I tried this. Without this general knowledge from the past I definitely would have to rely on expensive control systems. I rebuilt that machine six times. It is about the speed of the cooling water, the pressure of the cooling water, how many gallons a minute, the preheating of the drum, the temperature of the wax, avoiding vortex conditions. There are so many different factors. You have to be a little bit of a mechanic technical freak to do it. We cannot just talk about organic, natural, all of these nice things, we still need process control. For many people process control is a bad word—if you want to be really natural then you have to be a bee hunter in the woods."

He has met strong resistance to his frames from what he calls "the system." Hans-Otto explains, "The first years they were laughing at me. The same people that were laughing in 2002 and 2003 are now requesting frames with no stretching." He has tested the success of his frames over the past six years with striking results. But he is afraid to make them public. He has already been expelled from the Norwegian Bee Association for writing an article in *Bee Culture* magazine in 2005—an article simply showing positive results from the employment of natural cell size.

"I probably have to do it and take what's coming," he says, surrounded by papers, charts, graphs, a January 1934 edition of *Beeworld*, and pile of books dating back to 1760. "Because the beekeepers need it."

So he pushes onward against the consensus, the academic establishment, the professors and scientists who have much invested in the status quo, hundreds of them earning a living from the grants they received to find a solution, reluctant to kill the goose that laid the golden egg. These scientists have based their Ph.D. work on the notion of artificially enlarged hives, and bringing things back to the way nature intended, especially based on evidence from someone outside the scientific community, is a bitter pill to swallow.

"If scientists want to test this theory, fine, let them work! I'm just giving them a new idea. The problematic thing is that chemical companies are paying a whole lot of money into these university budgets where these professors and scientists get their income. That worries me. It's more or less like always—money, power, position. You're allowed to talk, you're allowed to talk . . . you, shut up."

And so scientists promote the use of drugs to combat the Varroa, all the while compromising the bee's ability to fight the virus itself, also killing good mites, scavengers that eat fungi and all the debris from the beehive, and a whole lot of other cooperating organisms. "When you knock out that whole population, it's like staying at a hotel and sending home the cleaning personnel. The scientists don't want to do those kinds of tests. It's the influence of the chemical regime. The mites are adapting to the chemicals, so they will continue to need new chemicals."

And it is about control. Norway is a socialist country. "Americans are in general more independent. If they want to make a decision, they make a decision. In Scandinavia things can be quite complicated because they like authority. They mentally like that somebody else is taking care of your problems. It's like walking into really wet marshland and you can't get your feet out. That's the situation. The professors can't speak out against the status quo too much. If they get into a situation where they aren't agreeing, their commando system will break."

In a country he lives in and loves, he chooses to step out of line; he is just that passionate about saving the honeybees. "There is one reason why I want to get this message out there. It is not for my fifteen minutes of fame. This is like putting a bullet in your own food. We will end up crashing."

He is having a hard time finding a way to make money from what he is doing. He is beginning to get orders from France for 5.1-millimeter-cell frames, the transition cell size, which indicates that some people are listening to him and reducing their cell sizes. Companies in Germany, Spain, and Sweden, though, are offering cheap frames, which keeps his margins small if he wants to compete. "Even though I have a better quality control system, my arguments have to be very good to get people to pay a little extra." He also sells pollen to body builders because it has efficient proteins. And he makes unique honey by mixing herbs like mint, thyme, and echinacea into it. "There's my little goldenroot test field," he says as we chug past a field of yellow bushes. He has been growing herbs in his yard for seven years, and testing many varieties of goldenroot to see what does and doesn't survive in this environment. He puts his honey in barrels for six months and lets the herbs soak in it, then strains out the big pieces. The flavor of the honey changes a lot from year to year. "When I eat honey for myself I eat clover honey right out of the bottle," he says. Heather honey harvested in autumn is the best-flavored honey, in his opinion, though he thinks wild raspberry honey is probably the most suitable for ordinary consumption. He produces comb honey, too, which he eats right from the comb.

Honey is a kind of element as pure as oxygen. It reflects the soil and climate in which it was made, moments in a plant's life. Bees collect a series of moments and put them together; a summary in a hive, then soon in a jar. It is the only food on the planet that never goes bad: it has been found in sealed clay pots in three-thousand-year-old Egyptian pyramids; it lasts forever.

Adding herbal remedies to his honey is a way of enhancing its natural beneficial properties, merely an extension of his holistic approach. "I'm a strong believer in nature and natural mechanisms. 'Biological optimization' is a very precise description of what I'm doing. Organic organizations don't pay attention to biological optimization. As long as they approve these acids and stuff it's totally pointless; organic has no meaning at all. I cannot talk about these things that are good for the body and then put a whole lot of crap into the beehives. It doesn't add up, it's impossible."

Hans-Otto spends July and August in a sleeping bag, moving his hives to the heather, *Calluna vulgaris*. He lives a simple life, one where he parks his car in the shadows to preserve his wax frames, where he converses with the Amish in America by letter and phone about special hand rollers.

"What I really like is being out with my tent and my truck and my sleeping bag," he says. "People tell me I'm a workaholic, but I enjoy it. I go to bed at night thinking about what I'm going to do the next day. It inspires me. In my engineering job they were always yelling, yelling. It's okay to be stressed, if I can choose my own stress." Men grow gray quickly in the dynamite-transporting business; but in the honey-transporting business they grow happy.

✒ BALSAMIC VINAIGRETTE

Among the most lauded recipes I have ever made is, of all things, dressing. "What is in this?" people ask, bright-eyed, from the table. "Honey," is the answer. A little honey makes everything better.

This vinaigrette is adapted from my grandmother Frances Pellegrini, though no matter how many times she tells me how to make it, mine is never the same as hers. It must be something in her kitchen air. She sometimes uses red wine vinegar instead of balsamic or a combination of the two and it works out just as well.

⅓ cup balsamic vinegar
1 tablespoon Dijon mustard
1 teaspoon honey
1 clove garlic
⅔ cup good olive oil
½ teaspoon sea salt
Black pepper to taste

In a blender, combine the vinegar, mustard, honey, garlic, and ¼ cup water. As you blend, add the oil in a thin, steady stream, incorporating the oil thoroughly as you go. An emulsified (homogenous) mixture will develop. Season with salt and pepper. Cover for a few hours to let the flavors meld.

MAKES ABOUT 1 OVERFLOWING CUP DRESSING

✴ GRANOLA BARS

This recipe is a guideline for proportions, but there is much flexibility in the ingredients you can use. I prefer to start with whole rolled oats rather than premade granola, as it is more natural and you have more control over the flavor. But if you want to make an even simpler version, you can use pre-made granola and reduce the baking time.

    3 cups whole rolled oats
    ¼ cup flax seeds
    ½ cup almonds, chopped
    ½ cup dried currants, cherries, or raisins
    1 teaspoon ground cinnamon
    ¼ cup (½ stick) butter
    ½ cup honey
    1 teaspoon vanilla extract
    1 ripe banana, pureed
    1 tablespoon fresh lemon juice
    2 large egg whites, lightly beaten

1. Preheat the oven to 350°F. Grease a 13 by 9-inch baking pan.
2. Combine the oats, flax seeds, almonds, currants, and cinnamon in a bowl and mix well.
3. In a small saucepan over medium heat, melt the butter with the honey and vanilla. Add the banana and stir.
4. Remove from the heat and pour over the oats mixture. Combine thoroughly, until all the ingredients are well coated. Stir in the lemon juice and then the egg whites.
5. Transfer the mixture to the pan and spread it out using the back of a large spoon to press it firmly and evenly into the pan. Bake for 25 to 30 minutes, until lightly browned.
6. Let cool completely. Cut into bars. Let the bars sit at room temperature, uncovered, for 24 hours to become firm. Afterwards store them in a sealed container or resealable plastic bag.

MAKES ABOUT 15 BARS

JON ROWLEY

The Taste Missionary

CHAPTER NINE

Seattle, Washington

Finding the Beautiful Taste

The oyster leads a rich and terrifying life. It spends its youth roaming as a freewheeling, miniature larva known as a spat, then grows one left foot and excretes a sticky gray, cement-like substance so it can attach itself to the first hard object it runs into. Its ability to commit to a personal pronoun, to call itself a he or a she, is uncertain from one year to the next. My relationship with the oyster was one of indifference until a seminal moment.

It arrived on New Year's Eve: a plain white box from Jon Rowley that offered no outer clue of its contents. The unsigned cream-colored note read, "Happy New Year. I like to think of oysters as a prelude to wonderful things about to happen." I systematically stripped back the layers of tape, plastic, and a blue vinyl cold pack, and sucked in the smell of brine. The package gave way to a heap of Totten Inlet Virginicas.

That night I discovered how to open an oyster well, finding the soft spot in the hinge and pressing a blunt knife down and then up until it gives way with a gentle popping sound. The oyster offers a quiet, graceful death and a lusty bit of gastronomical nourishment. My New Year's Virginicas were a mind-bending eating experience in which the soft meat, a little too large to take in one mouthful, makes you want to do it anyway because it fits so nicely in the pocket between the roof of the mouth and the tongue. The minced shallot and peppercorn accoutrements prickle the taste buds as the lump slides down the throat in a gentle finale.

⸺

The red sun is setting over the western horizon at the southern tip of Puget Sound, in the northwestern part of Washington state, ushering in the golden hour. Jon and I wait, watching the sun, popping oysters and thinking about them while we chew, taking in the serenity and gentle rhythm of the rocking fishing boats. His round face and focused eyes watch as he cuts the holding muscle between an oyster and its shell, the pink light reflecting on his bowl of white hair.

"They're alive up until you shuck them?" I ask with the oyster in my mouth.

"They're probably alive while you eat them," he says, looking for skipping rocks. "That's what gives them their vibrancy." I promptly swallow the oyster with some white wine, the cool liquid and the tepid meat conspiring in my throat as Jon throws a rock across the surface of the water.

Jon's own seminal moment came when, at the age of nineteen, he began a personal odyssey, hitchhiking from his high school graduation in Oregon to the Pacific Coast, where he hopped aboard a derelict seine boat to Alaska. From there he eventually made his way to Europe, where, after reading Hemingway describe an oyster in *A Moveable Feast*, he spent all the money he had on his first plate of oysters in a Parisian bistro. It was there that he experienced what he calls his first "oyster moment," and it drove him to spend his days haunting the fish stalls of French markets. There he learned the different names of the oysters and the numbering system by which they are sized. He continued his pilgrimage to the Belon River estuary in southern Brittany, and to the Charente-Maritime in Marennes, then to the vast oyster displays in Rungis, the sprawling market of Paris. He traveled to Spain, Portugal, and Norway to see how their fisheries worked. He went to the coastal fishing communities of New England. And then, after a brief stint at Reed College in Oregon, which he left before graduating, he bought a small boat and drove it back up to Alaska.

Jon fished for a decade, taking winters off to travel to Europe, where he'd go out on fishing boats and offer a free hand so he could see how the fisherman cooked and handled fish. He developed an esoteric knowledge of all things seafood. And then in 1980, a family tragedy altered his course. He sold his boat and hitchhiked back to Seattle.

In Seattle he began quietly changing the way America eats seafood. In the years leading up to this point, he kept asking himself how he could make the fish in America taste as good as the fish in Europe. He heard that a restaurant named Rossellini's 610 was serving superior fish and, excited, he went and ordered lingcod. But he could smell it from across the restaurant as it made its way to his table. He sent it back and asked to speak to the manager, who turned out to be the owner, Robert Rossellini.

But Rowley is not a renegade. He just loves the taste of things done well. He has a Garrison Keillor cadence to his voice that reflects an innocence and simplicity. He cares, and doesn't consider that anyone else wouldn't. He will tell you slowly and methodically without charisma or hyperbole the way things ought to be. And you will want to listen.

That night, Robert Rossellini listened until dawn. They started their conversation at the 610 and continued until it closed, then moved to Rossellini's legendary 410. They ended up at the Other Place, Rossellini's showcase restaurant. The wine kept coming out of the cellars, the vintages descending into history. And by sunrise, self-assured from the flight of vintage wines, Rowley agreed to teach Rossellini what good fish tasted like. More important, he set off on a path—a crusade, really—to improve the quality of fish brought to the American table.

With genuine passion and honest determination, he began to change the way the fisherman of the Pacific Northwest handled their fish. He asked his fisherman friends to first bleed the fish by opening an artery, stun them so they don't flop on the deck and bruise their flesh, then ice them immediately in the shallow stackable boxes he had seen in Europe, rather than piling them in a fish hold.

Rowley didn't stop there. To ensure that the better-quality product was properly transported all the way to the customer's table, Rowley went into restaurant kitchens around the country and taught cooks how to handle and cook fish, taught waiters how to sell it, and designed seafood grocery counters to properly display it.

He subsequently led the way in introducing the Copper River King salmon to the lower forty-eight states, and then went on a mission, literally knocking on doors like a hopeful politician, to bring back the only oyster native to the Northwest, the Olympia oyster. Up until this point, the Olympia was something no one had seen outside of a jar.

The fishermen had lamented poor fish prices but had no idea how to improve their situation. Rowley knew that if he persuaded them to handle the fish properly on the boat, their circumstances might change. They resisted, but after time agreed to give it a try. Rowley had Alaska fisherman load three hundred pounds of Copper River King on Alaska Airlines with the first spring run of the 1983 season. He drove in the middle of the night to pick the fish up and delivered them to restaurants as early as he could. "I spent a lot of time working with staffs in kitchens and trying to have them understand how to work with the fish, how to respect it. In every restaurant where I did that, there was a kind of infectious result. The effect of a beautiful piece of food, it sends reverberations through a restaurant. It inspires kitchens. It takes a really good chef to just leave good ingredients alone."

Eventually came crab, abalone, and spot prawns, which he also sold directly—illegally—to restaurants. He had to pay his fishermen cash because the health department wouldn't grant him a license. But the customers went wild.

"My primary motivating factor is taste," he says to me one morning, holding a bag of Shuksan strawberries in the air. "This will give you a taste of what I do." He hands me a strawberry. "They are only good for one day." And the taste of this strawberry, on this day, is like eating a strawberry for the first time.

Though his pursuit of beautiful taste started with fish, Rowley then began what he calls a seven-year journey of curiosity. "I wanted to know how two foods growing in basically the same place could have such different results. What is that all about? That question led me away from fish."

On any given Saturday you will find Jon Rowley roaming a farmers' market with his "truth machine," a refractometer that calculates brix, a measure of sucrose concentration. He squeezes a drop of fruit onto the glass dish and thoughtfully observes the results. This is how he pursues quality—diligently, academically, and without compromise. "Anywhere I could get a drop of juice out of things, I did. It gave me an understanding," he says, recalling his fixation. He became a compulsive note taker, and wrote down thousands of brix measurements and their sources. When he finds someone who has really good stuff he visits the farm to find out why it's so good by looking at their whole farming program.

———

My first lesson in brix begins at Jon's breakfast table over a plate of scrambled eggs and Swiss chard, which he grows in a converted parking strip on the sidewalk. He offers up the first ripe tomato of the year and hands it to me so I can feel the warmth of the sun on its skin. He drops some of its juice on the refractometer and peers through the microscope—a five. A really good tomato is a six, he says. Then he gets out a pair of Frog Hollow peaches, which are delivered to his house weekly because he has concluded that they are the best in the country. He knows this because he went on a two-year quest to find the best peach after convincing a grocery chain to pay him for it in his role as taste consultant. He hands me the refractometer to peer through the lens and show me that the peach's brix is off the charts.

"In the interest of science," he takes me to Chinooks, a restaurant by the water, and orders a blackberry cobbler. He invented this dish for them when he served as their consultant years ago, because the wild blackberries he discovered were spectacular. He waits for them to ripen every year and has people on the lookout, ready to inform him when they have peaked. The cobbler arrives, steaming warmth and the smell of briar. "This variety is Rubus ursinus. Can you taste the briar?" he asks. But they have added too much sugar to the blackberries, and the sweetness is cloying. He shakes his head, "Sugar is cheaper than fruit, which is why fruit desserts are often too sweet. That's what a guy who processes fruit told me. The number-one criterion is whether you taste sugar or fruit in the aftertaste," he says. "I taste sugar."

But then he moves on. "Do you like purslane?" I do, but usually as an accent in green salads, not by itself. And so he sets about changing my mind, collecting the weed from his garden, picking the fleshy leaves, and tossing them with sweet onion and tomato chunks, salt and pepper, and a little bit of juice squeezed from the tomato. "I like really simple foods," he says. "This doesn't need any dressing other than a little juice from the tomato." And as we sit for dinner over a plate of purslane salad, and the next night too over a plate of parsley and anchovy paste and beautiful bread, I become a convert. This is what he has done all his life: change people's minds. He's a kind of taste missionary.

Rowley likes to go to the farmers' market early, before it opens, so he can take pictures and visit with the friends he has made at virtually every stall. He carries his refractometer with him, tasting cherries, checking their brix, and giving a young farmer a lesson in how to measure when he looks wide-eyed at the apparatus. "Old Billy there has to get his brix up on his tomatoes. He's watering them too much," he says. He gets out his refractometer to show me. These lusty tomatoes are only a five. "They look good, though, don't they? Farmers used to call me the brix police. Now a lot of them have a refractometer. I don't know why restaurants don't have them. It's a truth machine." Brix measures the success of the plant, more than the sugar content. A high brix tomato won't taste sweet necessarily but will taste more like a tomato and have a denser texture.

The Ballard farmers' market in Seattle is beginning to awaken. Stalls line the street, teeming with plump eggplants and fertile eggs. "Hello, citizen," says a wiry, white-bearded man wearing shades and a hoodie. Then he recognizes Jon and illuminates. He gives Jon a little package in exchange for cash in what looks like some kind of drug deal. Jon gives the package to me—it is Washington state saffron.

Then he honors my request to taste raw milk, which can be sold legally in Washington. He buys two kinds, goat and cow. It tastes clean, pure, light, crisp, with no metallic aftertaste. As I revel in the milk, he visits with garlic farmers he doesn't know. He tells them his garlic has just come up. "You grow garlic?" they ask. "Yeah, in my parking strip," he says.

We collect Kumamoto oysters, ingredients for ratatouille, and blueberries for pie. He tells me to commit to just one kind of berry. "Mixed berry" usually means that none of the berries is good enough to stand on its own. You can't enjoy any single berry's flavor.

Soon in his kitchen, I stir a pot of ratatouille, which, now converted, I willingly flavor with anchovy paste. "Angelo Pellegrini used to tell me that was his secret ingredient," he says of the legendary food writer (no relation to me). Tasting spoons are scattered around the kitchen for all of the canned fruits, apple butters, and chutneys he has opened for us to try. From around the country, people send him their food inventions for approval, for his seal of good taste.

He has a note from Julia Child on his fridge, and a big picture that he took of her, in his office near filing cabinets that, instead of being labeled A–Z are labeled Snapper–Sole, Oysters, Mussels, Clams, Salmon, Umami, Flora and Fauna, Soil. He is private about his friendship with Julia, reluctant to use it as a means for attention. But as he shucks the Kumamotos he says, "I've seen her suck down six dozen oysters. I had oysters with her a few times, with Jacques Pépin and a few others, and she left us all in the dust. She had no patience for bad oysters but she loved good ones. I used to send them to her every Valentine's Day and ask her to be my valentine. Julia had encouraged me when I didn't know where my path was."

He also sent her Frog Hollow peaches every year for her birthday. She made sure he sent enough for her family, who gathered at a resort in Maine every year to celebrate her birthday and was characteristically good about sending juicy reports of how much they were enjoyed. In her last years, Julia, unable to travel, lived in an assisted-living facility in Santa Barbara, and Jon kept sending her the peaches. The day before she died he called her and asked, "Julia are you going to want your birthday peaches?" "'Yes, yes,'" he says, imitating her sing-song voice, "'send the peaches.'"

John recalled, "I heard the news shortly after she died. It was an emotional moment. It was late in the afternoon. The sun would be setting soon. I grabbed my camera and drove for twenty miles to this spot on the Strait of Juan de Fuca where I could get a shot of Julia's last sunset. I arrived just in time." That night he set a place for her at the dinner table. He knew she was there.

Slate-blue Kumamotos are scattered before us, and we chew them thoughtfully, sipping the last drops of this year's oyster wine winner (yet another one of Jon's projects), Chateau Sainte Michelle 2008 Pinot Gris. In the Kumamoto, the flavor elements touch every part of the palate, from the sweet, to the earthy, to the salty sensors on the tongue. For this reason he says it is better to be an oyster chewer, not a swallower. "How can you taste it? What's the point?" he asks sincerely.

We wait for the flavors of the ratatouille to marry, and make his dog Lady brown rice and salmon for dinner. "I grew up with two alcoholic parents," he says, stirring a pot and doting on Lady. "I remember escaping from the house with a sleeping bag, a skillet, a cube of butter, and salt and pepper. I was always out camping, fishing, spending time on the beaches, having kid adventures. I basically spent my whole life trying to get away from my childhood, then trying to retain certain aspects of it. I did this really so I wouldn't have to get a job," he smiles. "I learned at a certain point that I had a knack for making other people money and making chefs more successful at what they do. Sometimes it's hard for people to see what I'm doing; I go about it a little differently."

We talk into the night, full of ratatouille and Kumamotos, aged charcuterie, and interesting cheese. Before too long, I fall asleep and am awakened by the smell of an apple pie. Kate McDermott, Jon's wife, is preparing a lesson in pie.

I descend into the kitchen as Kate pulls her apple pie out of the oven and asks me to listen to it, to put my ear close to the surface and let the song tell me if it is done. I close my eyes and listen; it makes the vibrating sound of a low, heavy heartbeat, and the sound of lips smacking.

Jon decides to participate in pie class for the first time. He is making "anniversary pie," for today is their anniversary. Kate, a pianist by trade, launches into an elegant lesson on pie making, conjuring images of days on the prairie when there was little time, lots of children, and things to do. "Think up!" she says again and again as we fluff the lard and flour in our parted fingers. "Be the pie, Jon, be the pie," she says as he struggles with his dough. We mold our dough into "chubby disks" and let them chill while we go to pick blackberries in a patch Jon has been eyeing. "This is what makes a pie taste good," he says, filling his bucket at a nimble pace. Then we return to roll our chubby discs, back and forth, back and forth, as I watch the spiders crawl to the top of the berry pile at the sink.

Soon my ear is picking out the crackling sound of blueberry, the bubbling of two blackberry pies, and the gurgling of huckleberry pie. Kate sits in the sun with a pitcher of lemon water, surrounded by pies, reading aloud a church sermon on apple pie from 1862 by Henry Ward Beecher. She opens two old apple books and leafs through the pages, musing on the hundreds of varieties. "The Swaar Apple from New York is the best," Jon interjects. "It is one of the ugliest and best apples I have seen and tasted." Jon and Kate went on a three-and-a-half-year quest to make the perfect apple pie. At one time they have had four hundred pounds of heirloom apples in their basement in their dedicated "apple refrigerator," and as she reads me their notes from years past on the mix of apples they have used in a single pie (ten or more), and as I take big bites, I conclude it is indeed the Holy Grail of apple pies. Jon continues his apple musings: "Anything less than an average of thirteen-brix apples is an inadequate pie," he says. "And some apples taste better with age." But I have already drifted to the land of chewing, every bite a fruitful adventure, different than the one before.

They insist that I attend their anniversary dinner, and soon I sit at a waterside restaurant learning the proper way to eat Dungeness crab and hearing the story of how they met. Jon takes away my crab-cracking tools and shows how to crack with my fingers. He says that if a Dungeness crab is properly prepared, one should need only hands. We harvest the crabmeat with our fingertips, and Kate tells me that Jon courted her with compost. "I was looking for answers to improve my soil, and he had them." He arrived with his blue suspenders, and not long after attended her piano recital, after which he said, "I have some flowers for you. I'm going to get them. They're in the back of the car." He opened the back of the car and brought out a baggie of compost and presented it to her.

"These are composting roses of every shade of pink, ten thousand of them," he said.

"And I went weak in the knees," Kate says with a giggle, "and thought, He doesn't have to do another thing."

———

The next day I sit eating pie with the mailman. It has reached 102°F in Seattle, the hottest day in the city's recorded history, and Kate has invited him in as she always does, to partake in the five pies. "FedEx is gonna have some pie, too," Jon announces, pleased, as he escorts a bewildered-looking FedEx worker to the table.

Having scraped the last vestiges of blueberry from my plate, Jon asks if I want to see some fish. In order to master fish cookery, Escoffier would have his cooks make Dover sole over and over and over again until they understood how simple it really was. "There's a way to coax the best out of fish," Jon says. "I spent a lot of time watching the Indians cook fish. They cook on a latticework of cedar sticks next to a coal fire so they get even, radiant heat."

Ten minutes from Jon's kitchen, we arrive at the fish market, where we press the salmon bodies and feel for the firmest one. We look to see which has the most scales intact and which has that aspic-like slime on the body that forms during rigor mortis. According to his "Rigor Mortis Theory," the best-tasting fish is one that has gone through rigor mortis and comes out of it before it is eaten. A fish can actually be too fresh. The flesh of the fish should have that limpid quality, a vivid transparency. We go along and he quizzes me, telling me to pick the best fish in the bunch. He trades the fishmonger for an apple pie and we leave with a Yukon Chum salmon and a Yukon King salmon, the latter an extraordinary find.

In his kitchen, Jon oils the fish and lays it in a dry skillet, scorching it a bit so it is well browned. Then he turns it, and puts it in an oven preheated to 200°F. "I'm a fan of slow-cooking salmon," he says. When a salmon has a lot of oil, which it often does, too much heat makes the oil break. The strange white goo that sometimes appears is albumen, and represents a tissue breakdown, which means the fish or cooking execution has been less than perfect. Very good quality fish or preparation means you will never see that. And if the fish is too fresh, it will go through rigor mortis in the pan: the body will contract and distort, tearing the cell walls and excreting the albumen.

"That's my vote for the best fish in the ocean," Jon says of the Yukon King. "They have to swim over a thousand miles to spawn, which creates a lot of oil." While he cooks, Kate packs me a container of leaf lard so I can create a pie of my own. Jon hands me a refractometer so I, too, can learn the truth behind the country's fruit.

As I leave, I keep thinking about Jon's article on umami, a concept he spent seven years studying. Umami is a Japanese word that can't be directly translated into English. It encompasses all of the senses: sight, smell, touch, hearing, and taste. "A food has umami when it has become all that it can be, when it is at its peak of quality and fulfillment," he says. It is that beautiful taste that balances on a fine line for a fleeting period of time before it is gone forever.

His notes still arrive daily with thoughts on how to improve our ratatouille with more anchovy, how to give the pie crust a stronger "backbone," a greeting from the oyster beds where he is taking photographs. I can still taste the mineral finish of the Virginica and see him intently listening to a Bartók quintet playing at a fever pitch, reaching its violin climax and ending in radio applause as he claps, too. Five days of seeing the world through his eyes is an education that no one can get behind the ivy walls. They were the best eating days of my life, where I first encountered the beautiful taste.

———

🌿 PURSLANE SALAD

As seen at Jon Rowley's dinner table.

Purslane is a fleshy weed that grows in sidewalk cracks and gardens. It is also available in farmers' markets, where you may find both the wild and the slightly milder domestic variety. It contains more omega-3 fatty acids than any other leafy vegetable, and has an extremely potent nutritional value. It also tastes very good if you know how to use it. I didn't use it properly until Jon Rowley made me realize that I do like it as more than just an "acid accent" in my usual mixture of salad greens. He and I share a love of simple foods, with very simple ingredients. This salad is just that. The acid and sweetness from the onion, tomato, and purslane create a perfect balance—taste and add more of one or another as necessary. Serve the salad with good bread, cheese, and charcuterie.

Purslane, tougher stems removed, washed
Tomatoes, cut into chunks
Sweet onion, cut into chunks
Salt and black pepper to taste

Combine all of the ingredients, squeezing the juice of the tomatoes onto the salad to give it a little extra "dressing." That is all you need, and it is divine.

MAKES 1 BIG SALAD

✔ SALMON À LA JON ROWLEY

When you cook salmon the Jon Rowley way, it results in a piece of fish that is evenly cooked and very tender throughout.

1 (1-inch-thick) salmon steak (King salmon, if you can get it)
    or 1 piece of skin-on salmon fillet
1 tablespoon good olive oil
Salt and black pepper to taste

1. Preheat the oven to 200°F.
2. Heat a dry skillet until quite hot.
3. Brush both sides of the fish with oil and season both sides with salt and pepper. Place the fish in the skillet (flesh side down, if using a fillet), until the meat is bronzed, 1 to 2 minutes. Turn it over and brown the other side, then transfer the skillet to the oven and roast for about 10 minutes more, until tender and juicy but cooked through.

MAKES 1 PERFECT PORTION

KAREN WEINBERG

The Cheese Shepherd

CHAPTER TEN

Shushan, New York

Between Sky and Earth, There Is Cheese

I t is overcast in Shushan, New York. Farms stand paralyzed, some partly collapsed, some bearing crooked shutters. There is an occasional tractor on the road, and an occasional random store—one with carved wooden bears of many sizes, another with a dirt bike suspended in the air. The hills seem to lead to nowhere; a lone black cow has her head thrust through a hole in a tattered barn along a narrow road, her long face almost close enough to lick the passing cars. She is the only sign of life for miles, until the moment you feel utterly lost. Then a diminutive sign emerges and you are actually there—at 3-Corner Field Farm.

At the end of a gravel driveway, Karen Weinberg is sitting on an overturned bucket spraying blue paint onto the head of a baby lamb, a marker that will help her make sure it is nursing. With her overalls and efficiently short hair, she stands with a thin smile and preoccupied face. The air in the barn, sweet-smelling and moist, is filled with a chorus of sheep noises, different notes coming from different-size sheep, with an occasional exclamation from a nervous rooster. She puts the squirming lamb back into the "jug," a metal pen filled with alfalfa hay. She says to it,

"You're not the best in show, are you, but you're cuter than a button."

It is lambing season. New lambs are born every day, sometimes twelve in a day. Karen starts work at six o'clock in the morning, and, aside from an occasional coffee break, usually doesn't finish until three the following morning. "My husband says he's seen me fall asleep while I chew," she says, sitting now on an overturned milk crate bottle-feeding a lamb.

Lambing is the hardest time of year—it is when the animals are most vulnerable. "For a couple of weeks, it's very intense. In some ways it's the worst part of the job, but this is also my chance to re-bond with them." This is the only time in their lives that the sheep are in a barn. It is when Karen can manage a bad hoof or a missing ear tag. And as new ones are born, Karen helps the mothers dry them off, and dips the umbilical cords. She puts the babies in the jug and helps them bond with their mother by showing them how to nurse. She tags their ears and logs them into a book—"9210 goes with 9060." She vaccinates them all with vitamin E and selenium, and if any are sick, she gives them medication. In essence, Karen is a ninja midwife for six weeks every year.

She has an intimate knowledge of the sheep, and quickly learns the traits of the new ones arriving daily. She refers to them as "little tiny munchkins"; she talks to them, listens to what they have to say. "What?" she says to an old ewe. "You're missing all your teeth, how do you graze?" She clips an extra ear tag on one of the ewe's female lambs. "She's an old-timer. She's been with us for nine years. She's one of our better milkers, and she's the last of her line, so we want to make sure we keep track of her offspring. And she's a very attentive mom. Some of them are real good mothers; others need a little more time."

Karen separates the first-time mothers from the older ones because they are more flighty. She gives them a chance to learn good mothering by letting them interact with their lambs without interference. New mothers will sometimes walk away from their newborns because they don't understand what is happening. By separating them, Karen can help the experienced ewes give birth without influencing the new mothers.

In the orphan jug, curly-haired lambs of various miniature sizes are bouncing around, lapping up warm molasses water and discovering the electrical cord to chew on. This jug is where lambs go whose mothers couldn't handle feeding a third lamb or who died giving birth. Karen lifts one up with a green spray-painted head and examines her tight round belly. It is extended because she drank too much sweet water to curb her hunger. Karen stops her from drinking it. "Green head is feisty. Somehow she decided that this was an okay substitute." Karen lifts her out of the jug and tries to feed her milk-replacement formula with a bottle, but she is resisting, she knows the difference. "If she gets hungry enough, she'll drink it. Last night she was so hungry she drank half a bottle and she didn't even care." Karen remembers these details for all 350 lambs in the barn, and their 150 mothers.

The room reverberates with noises that sound like "Ma." A mother calls to her baby in the orphan jug and the baby calls back. Karen notices—she speaks their language, and she knows, almost as well as they do, who belongs to whom. "That one over there has a fog horn," she says. "Those are people," she says to the lamb calling its mother. The mother "bah"s at her. "I know that's your baby." She reunites them and tries to figure out why the ewe isn't letting her babies nurse. "Is that your baby?" she listens with a sixth sense. "She's got a way big udder." She climbs into the jug, gets on her knees, and milks one of the teats by hand. Three lambs run around her in circles, trying to push their way to the milk; the mother tries to resist. Karen gets twisted up and braces herself against a post to get a good grip.

"It's okay, Mom," she says softly. "She's way too full. She's one of our better milkers so I know that if she's not letting them milk there's something wrong." Then returning to the lamb, "I can't do it with my other hand, sweetie; you love this hay, I know you do." She notices the ewe has some blood in her milk because her udder is engorged. "It must feel a lot better, huh, Mom?" One of the babies wiggles its way to the second udder and finishes Karen's work for her. The ewe relents and Karen dresses the sores on her udder, which she thinks were caused by the baby's teeth.

Ewes can have one to three lambs at a time. And, like cats, they can be bred with more than one father at a time. Most of the adults on the farm are crossbred, but the predominate strain is East Friesian, which is a milking breed, combined with heartier breeds known for producing stockier meat and good wool. The Lacaune is also incorporated—the French breed from whose milk Roquefort cheese is made.

Karen purposely plans lambing for the spring. The ewes are shorn in March, and they are finished lambing just as the grass is coming in, so they can go to pasture in May and teach their lambs how to graze. If lambing happened in winter, the lambs would never have a chance to be outside on pasture and learn from their mothers.

The milk supply is also optimal when the sheep are grazing. Three Corner Field Farm practices rotational grazing, which means the animals are moved on a daily basis. This is financially advantageous since the sheep are eating grass, and their manure fertilizes the fields. It also means there is considerable work involved—moving mobile fencing and hauling water to remote locations.

At pasture, the sheep nibble on the newest, sweetest, most tender growth because they don't have upper teeth. "Sheep don't digest food by chewing it," Karen says. "They digest food by ruminating it. All they care about is taking it in as fast as possible. Then when they're done taking it in, they will more leisurely regurgitate and ruminate it, and that's part of their digestive process. And so when you put them in a new pasture with really good grass, they'll race around and eat as fast as they can, then they'll sit down and ruminate it."

She could feed all of the animals in one hour in the barn versus the six hours it takes when they are all on pasture. Out in the field they have to have water pumped out to them, two hundred gallons per day. In the barn the water automatically refills by itself. So there are real efficiencies to having them all in a confined space. "There's a reason that modern agriculture developed. But it doesn't give the animals a real life. It's one thing to decide we're going to use them for food; it's a whole other thing to torture them in the process. We have ewes that have been producing for us for ten years. I can only compare it to cows in industrial settings: they're in the barn all the time being fed concentrate, and hormones, and producing constantly. The average lifespan in that environment is three to four years for a cow, but in a natural setting a cow will last twelve to fourteen years. It's like a machine that wears out from being used all the time. And most of the modern barns have lights on all the time, because they discovered that the cows will produce more when it's light. So the cows are never in the dark. We're far less efficient, that's for sure. And we probably make a lot less money. I could handle this farm myself if everyone was kept in the barn. But if you're going to take responsibility for all these animals, part of treating them well is giving them the life they're supposed to have. So what if you made a little bit of money but you took shortcuts and you made bad decisions in order to do that."

Karen and her husband, Paul Borgard, have known each other since they were thirteen. Paul says she has talked about having a farm since they first met, and she says it started long before that. But they spent most of their adult lives in a city, inside the confines of corporate life—Karen has a Ph.D. in statistical analysis, and Paul had a career with GE. They kept a few sheep at their country home as a hobby, and to keep the grass short, but after returning from a three-year stint in Paris they were inspired to move to the country full-time.

"It sort of evolved," Karen says. "I didn't quite know what I was getting myself into, but this is what I always wanted. When we were in France we had a lot of sheep's milk cheese, and we thought, Wow, if we're going to have sheep, why not have the best of everything? It's a small, easily manageable animal. They herd really easily. They move almost as far as you can see in every direction with a Border Collie. I had a young daughter, and sheep are pretty docile animals—they're good to have around kids." So within three years, Karen and Paul went from 4 to 167 sheep.

Now they invest a lot of money in nourishing all of them. Producing milk takes more calories than almost anything in mammals, and because the sheep are milkers they are milking outside the normal lactation curve and have higher nutritional demands. In the middle of May, Karen will start weaning the first set of lambs—she will simply take the moms into the milking parlor and let the lambs continue grazing the way their mothers taught them. She will have let the lambs nurse for longer than modern commercial farms because it produces healthier animals in the long run and because waiting to wean them means the milk is higher in solids and fat. "The death rate of lambs that are weaned early is astronomical, upwards of 40 percent," she says. "Most commercial dairies now sell the lambs as soon as they're a day old. They want them out the door as soon as possible so they can start milking the mothers, even if they get only five bucks for them."

Karen and Paul are thoughtful about the choices they make and the tangled relationship between ethics and economics. They keep twenty-five to thirty lambs for milking every year and since they don't need the other 350 to be milkers, they breed them to have different qualities—some are stocky and good for meat, some, like the Persians and Border Leicesters, have interesting wool or beautiful fleeces, some have skin good for tanned hides. All of these are products they can sell at farmers' markets to make the money they need to give their animals a certain quality of life.

This efficiency is necessary as they think about the cost of raising the animals and the income needed to continue in this way. And in turn, the food and quality of life they invest in the animals inherently affects the quality of all of the products they sell. It is a perfect self-fulfilling cycle. Almost no parts of the animals are wasted. Offal goes to chefs, bones are sold for stock, some of the wool goes to the man who shears the sheep to help offset the costs of shearing, and the rest is sold to be spun. If they sold their lambs right away, it would be much clearer where most of their money was coming from, and they would make more of it. But they spend a lot nourishing the lambs used for meat, and they aren't in a rush to sell them; they are willing to keep them and invest in them until they are eleven months old, almost to the point where they are no longer officially lambs.

"We always tell people that we're better than organic," Karen says. "The animals are out on pasture. I don't ship them off when they get sick just to say that I'm organic. If my animals get sick I treat them with antibiotics the way I would my children." She says this as she mixes warm and cold molasses water to get the right temperature and systematically makes her way around the barn to refill each bucket. "A lot of the choices we made were defined by experience. I don't want to do this job if I know every year, after putting all of this effort into the quality of their lives, that their last two days were horrendous because I sold them off at auction. You don't know how you're going to feel until a difficult moment happens. Somebody could replicate what we did here by copying the decisions we made but they wouldn't necessarily know why we made those decisions. This is our tenth year of making those decisions." A ewe sucks down the whole pail of molasses water and waits for more. Karen laughs and refills it.

As devoted as she is to her sheep, she is candid about what it means to be an omnivore in a society with so many food choices. For example, telling people that somehow no animals die in the process of making cheese is dishonest. The meat, milk, and cheesemaking systems all fit together beautifully in a balance that is centuries old: the ruminates that are producing the milk produce the offspring, which produce the stomachs that are taken after slaughter to make the rennet that makes the cheese. "This is what it takes to make cheese. My big pet peeve is when people who will eat cheese won't eat meat or will only eat cheese using "vegetarian" rennet. You can slice and dice and rationalize all you want and if you want to pretend that cheesemaking is not related to meat production or that animals aren't killed in order to have dairy, then you can live in your fantasy world but it is not the real world."

From the cheese room Karen can watch her husband milk the ewes. There are lanes in the barn that lead to the milking parlor. The ewes drink water while they wait, then come in twelve at a time and eagerly take their place because they know a bit of grain is waiting for them. Feeding them a small amount of grain excites them and keeps their body condition up because it is something new, which means they will eat more calories.

The automatic feed slowly nudges them backward so that their tail ends meet the milking jars. The room fills with the grassy smell of grain, and Paul walks back and forth, attaching and unattaching the milking tubes. The suction from the tubes makes a drumming sound that, despite the noise, sends the room into a peaceful mode. Paul, too, has an intimate knowledge of the sheep, but his perspective is quite different from Karen's. Whereas she knows them from the front, he knows them from behind. Trying to describe a particular ewe to each other is nearly impossible.

While the milking tubes drum, Karen is elbow deep in a vat of 92°F curd and whey from the morning milking. As she raises the temperature, more whey separates from the curd. With less whey, the cheese will keep longer. She pulls the curd up from the bottom and folds it back in. She breaks it apart with her fingers and works it until it is somewhat elastic. She is looking for the right balance so that the curd will knit together properly when she puts it in the molds. "I have a hard time imagining how you could get a feel for the whey in a big vat," she says, referring to mass-produced cheese. "Everything you do with cheese is pretty gentle and intuitive."

Outside the milking parlor is the washroom where Karen scrubs her equipment. She has a fastidious nature about her, and keeps things immaculate, especially the red rubber bottle nipples she uses to feed the lambs. A visitor named Ed arrives in the washroom to buy some yogurt. Ed lives in Queens, New York, but likes to stop in when he visits his house in the Adirondacks. He has a union job working on the *New York Times* press machines, and he knows a lot about food and is willing to go out of his way for the good stuff. "This is the best lamb I've had. The best flavor I've had," he says while waiting for his yogurt. "I would say fresh, and flavorful, not gamey. And that's from the grass. I really haven't had better—and I've shopped around."

Karen thinks the flavor is the result of a combination of things. "The dairy animals produce meat that is a finer grain and milder than the wooly breeds that have gamier meat. The grain of the meat is like filet mignon; the texture is fine, so even the cuts that aren't prime are tender. The flesh is milder than most lamb; the flavor is not overly strong."

"I've given this lamb to people who don't like lamb," Ed chimes in.

"And we feed them right, we don't stress them out, they get a good life," Karen adds. She is conscious of how serene the animals' daily environment is, which is reflected in the fact that many of her sheep give birth during the day. In farms where there is a lot of commotion sheep tend to give birth at night when there is quiet. A lot of their choices are based on instinct.

Karen hands Ed his two pints of yogurt, and he teases her. "This was an innocent little hobby that got totally out of control. What was it again, a couple of sheep to keep the grass cut?"

It is starting to rain in Shushan. We drive the farm cart along the road, herding the sheep from pasture, one slow old sheep lagging far behind, then soon toward the house past two sleeping, shaggy-haired sheep dogs, Roquefort and Manchego, and a Border Collie named Sweeps who, finished herding for the day, is chasing us from behind. Sweeps is a real-life Lassie: One day a woman working with some lambs down the road had accidentally let a group of them into the road. She called for help on the walkie-talkie. Somehow, Sweeps heard the woman's call over the walkie-talkie, knew who was calling and where she was. When Karen and Paul got there, Sweeps was already rounding up the sheep. "It was amazing," Karen says. "She knew that it was a call for help, and went there on her own initiative. The type of canine intelligence it takes to do that is incredible."

The sheep dogs are talented, too. They identify and socialize with the sheep so deeply they have an instinctive desire to protect them. They do their sleeping during the day, and at night patrol the fence line and kill anything they think is a threat. They learn how to communicate with the lambs and every year teach the new lambs that when they bark a certain way the lambs should respond accordingly.

Inside the 1840s farmhouse kitchen, Karen has a cast-iron stove that, before the days of fire codes, was partly wood burning. She warms a loaf of baguette au levain, a naturally risen, yeast-free bread made by her neighbor, who built himself a wood-fired outdoor brick oven. He is a purist, and it reminds her of her days in France. With the loaf in the oven, we descend into her cheese vault, which she fashioned from a nineteenth-century root cellar. It is made out of brick and well insulated. For seven months of the year the room is naturally the right temperature, 50° to 54°F, and 89 percent humidity, which produces a firm rind on her cheeses.

The room smells of ammonia. She carefully cycles the air, as too much will dry the cheese out. On the back wall are wheels of Frère Fumant, a washed cured cheese she has smoked with hickory for six hours by the monks of New Skete, New York, and which she named for Brother David, the monk who smokes it. The smoke renders the cheese leather-looking on the outside, like a well-polished shoe. On the ground, in buckets, sheep's milk feta is ripening. Large Pyrenees-style

Battenkill Brebis wheels sit on the opposite wall coated in mold, a result of the bacteria that gets added to the milk, and the natural condition of the old basement. Because it isn't smoked, the bacteria flourish more easily and flavor the cheese more intricately.

In the middle of the room is a bath where the cheese is brined in salted water, which helps produce a crust and extract the extra whey (whey has a lower pH and therefore higher acidity). Adding warm water is a way of aging the cheese. It reduces acidity and raises the pH, leaving more moisture behind and limiting the sharp tang that a cheddar would develop.

Karen also makes a sheep's milk camembert by adding penicillin to the milk. After the cheese is made, she puts it in a ripening refrigerator, at 54°F and 95 percent humidity. It is ripened for three to six weeks, and the chemical reaction with the mold gives it a sublime gooey texture. When she first began this business, she started with yogurt and fresh cheese only, which meant she had to pasteurize it. But all of the aged cheeses are made from raw milk.

Unlike in Europe, United States regulators require all raw milk cheese be aged for sixty days, a number Karen thinks is arbitrary. It also deprives U.S. consumers of a whole host of cheese flavors and varieties. USDA inspectors visit Karen on average three times a month. They arrive unannounced and have free access to everything. They go through her farm without permission and can take whatever they want as samples. She has to leave a key for them when she is not home.

"Their job is to find something wrong. And they will, and I won't take it personally. The irony with inspectors is that they don't really know a lot about cheese-making; they just know what they're supposed to look at so it would be easy to pull the wool over their eyes if I wanted to, because they look at the most obvious and stupid things. But I don't. I'm hoping our inspector is smart enough to look around and see that we're people who are keeping things clean and trying to make a good product. The other sad truth is that the things that make us sick are not the things that these guys are preventing. It's at the big plants where the amount of oversight is not as good versus the amount of volume they do. Not in these little custom places, not in my little dairy where you can stand in one place and see everything that's going on."

Karen and Paul are down-to-earth when they talk of small farms in the United States. They have, after all, started a small farm in a time when people are getting out of farming.

"Every six days another farm goes under," Paul says. "Or they've gone big, and now they can survive." But he thinks this life is viable for people looking for something more than their desk job. "If you're willing to lower your standards, take a step back, it can work. It's pretty tough to be a farmer. To go to the next level, we couldn't have done it if I hadn't worked for all those years and been willing to spend my savings as we moved toward profitability. The money that we make goes back into the farm. As a small family farm, you have to have a niche, but you also have to have capital and say, I'm spending this capital and I'm not looking back."

"You have to like the animal," Karen adds. "I've always liked sheep. They're good for pasture. They don't need big crop fields full of the best feed. They do fairly well on their own." And despite the demands of her new life Karen doesn't miss her corporate job. "You know, it's very hard work and sometimes it's very stressful. Like at the end of the lambing period three weeks of real stress and no sleep is very tough. But every once in a while someone will talk to me about going back to the corporate world or make me an offer, and it's not even something I consider. So that's how I know I'm in the right place."

✿ PARMESAN BROTH STEW

Cheese rinds have so much unrealized potential. When a good cheese has run its course the rind is there, waiting for its chance to show its glory, an opportunity it is too often denied. When there is nothing left in your kitchen but a few sad-looking things, you can use them and the rind to make some satisfying version of this stew.

> *1 tablespoon olive oil*
> *3 bulbs fennel, chopped*
> *3 ribs celery, chopped*
> *2 carrots, chopped*
> *6 shallots, chopped*
> *½ stalk lemongrass, chopped*
> *4 cloves garlic, crushed*
> *1 tablespoon fennel seeds*
> *1 teaspoon hot chile flakes*
> *Zest of 1 lemon, chopped*
> *6 sprigs fresh thyme*
> *1 bay leaf*
> *2 cups orange juice*
> *About 1 cup cheese rinds (Parmesan is good)*
> *Any vegetables you please: red onion, baby turnips, baby carrots,*
>   *leeks, Savoy cabbage, shiitake mushrooms, radishes, and so on*

1. Heat the oil in a large pot over medium heat and add the chopped fennel, celery, carrots, shallots, lemongrass, garlic, fennel seeds, hot chile flakes, lemon rind, thyme, and bay leaf. Sweat until the vegetables are just starting to soften, about 5 minutes.
2. Add the orange juice and enough water to cover the ingredients in the pot, then simmer for 2 hours, adding the cheese rinds halfway through.
3. Once the broth is full flavored, strain the liquid into another pot and discard the solids. Add the fresh vegetables and simmer until they're just tender.

MAKES ABOUT 2 QUARTS OF REALIZED POTENTIAL

✹ KEFIR

I have fond, peculiar memories of a glass jar sitting on the fireplace mantle, holding a liquid that constantly reinvented itself. It changed by the day, by the hour sometimes, from something strange to something more recognizable. This liquid, as it turns out, is intensely good for you, a drinkable yogurt full of good bacteria, and even better when flavored at the breakfast table with fruit purees. You can reuse the culture many times as a starter before you need to begin anew: 2 cups of kefir from a previous batch will ferment 1 quart of new kefir. It can be stored in the refrigerator for up to 12 months, and longer in the freezer. You can make kefir with coconut milk, rice milk, sheep's milk, goat's milk, or soy milk, but it won't get as thick as with cow's milk.

1 quart sheep's milk or cow's milk (whole)
1 (5-gram) package kefir starter culture (see Note)

1. Put the culture in a quart-size glass jar. Slightly warm the milk to about skin temperature and add it to the jar. Close the lid loosely, not airtight.
2. Place the jar on a mantle or another ledge of your choosing and watch the change slowly begin to happen. Time and temperature affect the thickness and flavor of kefir. In warmer temperatures it may be ready to drink in 18 hours; in cooler temperatures it will take longer—72° to 75°F is ideal. Left too long at room temperature, it will turn cheesy and sour, so finding the right amount of time is key. It should be creamy, like a drinkable yogurt, thicker than milk, with a sour perfume. Shake it well and refrigerate it once it has reached this pivotal state to slow down the culture.

Note: Starter culture can be found at health food stores or online.

MAKES ABOUT 1 QUART OF INTESTINAL GOODNESS

CUMIN-CRUSTED LAMB CHOPS

These lamb chops have a Middle Eastern flair, and are always a hit. You can add less cumin if you prefer a milder version. The fat from the chops blends well with the cumin. Serve them with Israeli couscous, parsley, and olive oil.

8 to 12 lamb chops or loins
3 tablespoons olive oil
½ cup ground cumin
1 teaspoon salt
½ teaspoon black pepper

1. Preheat the oven to 400°F.
2. Rub the chops with some of the oil. Combine the cumin, salt, and pepper and coat the lamb thoroughly with the mixture, using all of it. Drizzle the lamb with more oil and place the chops on a rack over a baking sheet, then in the oven. Roast for 12 to 15 minutes for medium-rare, turning the chops over halfway through.

SERVES 2 OR 3

✭ HOMEMADE CHEESE

Fresh cheese, also known as "drip" cheese, is simple to make and requires few ingredients. It has a neutral flavor and a soft, spreadable texture. This simplicity serves as a base for experimenting with added flavorings, and you can experiment with various milk types—sheep, goat, cow, and beyond.

> 1 quart whole milk
> Juice of ½ lemon, strained
> 1 pinch salt
> Pepper to taste
> Fresh herbs, garlic, spices (optional)

1. Combine the milk and salt in a saucepan and heat until the sides begin to bubble. Stir frequently so the milk doesn't scorch.
2. Remove from heat and add the lemon juice. Stir and let sit for 10 minutes so the curds form.
3. Place a piece of damp cheesecloth into a fine mesh strainer and set it over a large bowl.
4. Pour the curds and whey into the cheesecloth and strainer, and let the whey drain into the bowl.
5. Gather the four corners of the cheesecloth and tie them at the top with a length of kitchen twine. Hang the bundle of cheese over the bowl and let drip slowly for an hour or so until room temperature and firm. The less whey in the cheese, the longer it will keep.
6. Reserve the whey to use in baked goods.
7. Untie the cheesecloth, put the cheese into a bowl, and mix in salt and pepper. Add chopped fresh herbs, minced garlic, spices, or hot sauce for a variation. It will keep for about one week in the refrigerator.

Note: You'll need cheesecloth for this recipe; it's available in most grocery stores.

MAKES 1 CUP OF CHEESE

SUE FORRESTER

The Butter Poet

CHAPTER ELEVEN

Butter Poetry

For a moment I believe I have arrived at the home of a modern-day Beatrix Potter. I am in Cumbria, England. In front of me a house named Howberry appears. It is pink stucco with a white wrought-iron fence and an arch of wisteria vines growing above the entrance. Six ducks sit in front of the gate, quarreling.

Sue Forrester appears from the side of the house, and her round, ruddy face greets me with a pleasant look, her wispy white hair blowing in the breeze. Inside her kitchen, the buzz of an electric mixer drones. She moves about, clad in pastels, and affirms everything not once but three times: "Yes, mm-hmm, yeah."

In the kitchen, Sue has been pounding digestive biscuits with a wooden rolling pin and stirring them in a saucepan with butter. She is making lemon cheesecake, lots of it, patting the crumbly mixture with the back of a spoon and pressing it into the contours of ten aluminum pie tins.

She pours me coffee and places a pitcher of buttermilk crusted with cream on the pink tablecloth. I watch as she adds lemon jelly and the juice of two lemons to the cream rising in a cloud above the mixing bowl. I add buttermilk to my coffee and watch little lumps of it float. Sue's four-year-old grandson Charlie, peering above the rim of his thick little glasses, confides in me, "I've got a secret diary."

"And we have a head taster as well, don't we?" Sue announces as she removes the lemon cream from the mixer. Charlie nods and we both sample spoonfuls of lemon clouds while she pours the rest into the tins and smoothes the tops with a butter knife.

"I'm good at sticking them labels on," Charlie announces as Sue closes up the cake boxes. Then he requests chips for lunch.

Sue agrees and dutifully peels potatoes over the kitchen sink, pointing out a red-headed woodpecker through the casement windows. Outside, the ducks continue their quacking. "Ducks are part of our heritage," she says. "They eat slugs in the front yard and rule the roost."

Sue Forrester was born in Brompton, in northern England, her husband Tom in Carlisle a few miles south. They can trace their ancestry back through three hundred years of farming. They met at Young Farmers, the equivalent of America's 4-H Club, and have been married for more than forty years. They live on a small farm a few minutes from the three-hundred-year-old house in which she was born.

For most of their married life, Sue and Tom were dairy farmers in the low-lying plain that divides England from Scotland. They kept a Holstein-Friesian dairy herd, a breed that is most efficient at turning the area's abundant grass into milk. A two-person show, she and Tom milked their herd morning and evening, then Sue separated the butterfat from the buttermilk and produced a warm-yellow butter, all from the same little kitchen in which she cooks her meals.

But in February 2001, the outbreak of foot-and-mouth disease changed their lives. It started in Longtown, six miles up the road, and tore through the fields and barns, taking down much of the livestock in the region. As farms around them fell, Sue and Tom hunkered down and quarantined themselves, relying on their daughter to throw them groceries over the fence every few days, feeding their cows aloe vera, and keeping their fingers crossed. In the end they emerged as one of the few who evaded the outbreak.

Today in all of Cumbria, Sue is the only person who still makes her butter by hand. Now she gets her milk from down the street.

Too many neighbors needed cows, so she decided to sell them to simplify and focus entirely on making good butter. Sue usually makes butter two or three days a week and produces six to seven hundred pats of butter at a time using a lengthy process.

Making butter by hand is affected by temperature and weather conditions. When it is too hot during the day, she works in the middle of the night when the temperature is cooler. Each morning, wooden churns full of cream are delivered to the farm. She puts the cream into a large mixer and whisks gently for thirty to forty-five minutes, until the cream thickens. She stops intermittently to scrape down the sides of the bowl with her black-handled scraper. Eventually the cream separates into buttermilk and butterfat—the latter turns yellow and coagulates into the consistency of scrambled eggs sitting in a pool of translucent liquid.

Once most of the buttermilk has been worked out, she washes the mix in cold water to remove any remaining lactic acid, which causes it to spoil more quickly. When the water runs clear, she mixes in salt (for some batches), and beats it with wooden paddles to remove excess water. Then she weighs out 254-gram portions exactly (the extra 4 grams is to account for the small amount of liquid that lingers within and needs to be battered out of the butter during "patting"). She then shapes the butter with her wooden paddles to form it into rectangles. Sue uses old-fashioned wooden butter pats, called "scotch hands," to make the blocks. The rhythmical battering clatters the work surface as the butter is gradually pressed into shape. The sound she makes smacking them is exciting; it makes you want to dance. This rhythm seems to have inspired Sue as well over the years: she writes poems in her head while churning butter—long and clever ones that deal with a range of topics, from current events and politics, to rubber wellies (boots) and her grandsons. "When you're patting butter, your brain has to do something, doesn't it?"

When she is content with the result, she gives the top surface of each piece one last press and then marks it with her distinctive pattern before wrapping and labeling it. The horizontal line markings she uses as her seal were first introduced by her mother eighty years ago when she made butter in Haltwhistle.

"My mum was there the first day I made butter," she explains, gliding about her butter room in an apron, "and unprompted, adorned my first block of butter." Sue has used these markings ever since. The last aunt on Tom's side of the family soon introduced her family seal as well, which looks like an "X." In the days before mass packaging, it was typical to have a unique marking for your butter; it was a way for the consumer to remember their favorite butter by its distinguishing marks. And so her unsalted butter is distinguishable by the family "lines" and the salted butter is adorned with the family "X." She charges 1.30 pounds wholesale for a pat of butter, 1.60 pounds at the farmers' market.

Sue doesn't waste anything. The buttermilk left over is a special kind of buttermilk and different from what is available in modern supermarkets. In its natural, un-homogenized state it isn't cultured and thick. She uses it to make fruit loaves, tea breads, scones, and cakes, which she also sells. She has revived old recipes such as Grannie's Clipping Cake—a Cumberland cake with dried fruit, almonds, rum, and treacle (uncrystallized syrup produced in refining sugar). She now calls this treat "Coast-to-Coast Cake" because it provides a good carbohydrate rush when walking.

She also makes rum butter, one of the most traditional products of Cumbria used to celebrate christenings. The story goes that rum is the spirit of life, sugar is the sweetness of life, nutmeg is the spice of life, and butter is the richness of life. Traditionally, a mother-to-be made rum butter three months before the baby was due, keeping it under her bed until the baby arrived, when it was offered to visitors on oatmeal biscuits. Sue says her rum butter "sells by the cuddy load" (cuddy is Cumbrian dialect for "donkey").

Sitting at her kitchen table for evening tea, Sue feeds me a tomato sandwich on a spiced raisin bun loaf with butter, salt, and pepper, and she begins to recite some of her poems by heart. Negotiating the combination of tomato and raisin in my mouth, washing it down with Earl Grey tea and buttermilk, and listening to poetry in Cumbrian dialect is a pleasure I hadn't imagined existed.

There's a line of wellies.
From a little six to a big size ten.
Some are for the ladies and the rest
Belonging to the men.
The biggest ones are "down at heel"
With hayseeds and a pong.
These belong to Granddad,
Also known as Tractor Tom.
Jason's have a heavy tread
With a hint of lawn grass green.
Jane prefers the modern ones—
Gray with hoops of red and cream!
Lewis favours Spider-Man
On wellies black and neat.
And Charlie wears red Postman Pat
Quite often on wrong feet.
I have a pair of "cow pat green"
And a way-out pair with matching brolly.
But if I wear these 'round the farm
They think I'm off my trolley!
If you're aged from one to ninety-nine,
And wellies are your passion,
Be they plain or colourful
They'll be the height of fashion.

She ends each poem with a mischievous smile and a sip of tea.

This butter (and poetry) churning began because of European Union regulations that set a quota for milk production. Her small farm was over its milk quota, which meant that the Forresters would be fined for overproduction. But the cows still had milk in their udders, and they had to do something with it. So Sue skimmed the cream from the surface of her milk, swam through oceans of government red tape, and "Cream of Cumbria" butter began. What started in her kitchen, selling butter to her family and friends, has spread. Every Thursday she loads her van with pats of butter and makes her rounds, delivering to shops and inns along country roads across northern England.

In the early morning, Sue pulls up to my farmhouse lodging down the road in her navy Citroën with "Cream of Cumbria" emblazoned on the rear tire cover. We take off to deliver butter throughout the countryside, making our way from slick highways onto narrow country roads. The sheep in this region appear everywhere as white polka dots against the rolling green hills. Their fleece drags along the ground behind them in a woolen veil, because they aren't shorn in these colder parts until July. Miles of centuries-old stone walls partition the hills in random geometrical patterns to keep the grazing animals in their place. As we speed by, a cow lifts her tail and spouts pee into the air in a perfect arc.

We stop first in Penrith to visit Martyn Reynolds, who makes famous meat pies. Not long ago, Martyn was a policeman, then one day he decided that making pies was a better life. So now he spends his days in a white hairnet conjuring up new pies with interesting toppings. The room is filled with trays of steak pies; leek, onion, and cheese pies; pork and Stilton pies with gooseberries piled on top. He makes tiered wedding-cake pies, and heart-shaped pies with a shiny egg white finish. He methodically holds them up for me to see one by one alongside his wide grin.

Next, down a narrow side road past yellow gorse prickly bushes and bluebell woods, we come upon Churchmouse Cheeses in Kirkby Lonsdale, a town teeming with Springer Spaniels and knickers. There, John Natlacen sells cheese to the melodies of a pianist playing "Smoke Gets in Your Eyes" on an upright in the corner of the shop. A note beside him reads, "Please don't feed the pianist, he plays for peanuts." John once had a career in finance, but today he will make you a wedding cake out of cheese and wouldn't give this new life up for anything.

Farther northwest, in Ambleside, we stop at the Drunken Duck. The inn has been in business for four hundred years, but its name dates back only to the Victorian era, when one morning the landlady found several of her ducks lying dead by the road. She set about plucking them—only to discover that they were very much alive. A beer barrel in the basement had leaked into the ducks' feed, and they had merely passed out, drunk. So she knit them little jackets until their feathers grew back. We sit inside sipping beer and eating potted shrimp, smoked salmon, and pea and ham soup. "I couldn't live in a town," Sue says simply, dipping a thick-cut "chip" into a "drip" of ketchup and malt vinegar.

Up the western coast of the Solway Firth, where the microclimate changes by the minute from rain to sun, from cold to hot, we stop at the home of Annette Gibbons, a local food celebrity who knows all there is to know about Cumbrian food and takes people on "food safaris" to teach them about it. She lives by the Irish Sea, where she tends to her garden and two chickens. She is thrilled that she already has zucchini in May. Annette's tea room smells of African red rooibos tea. A window consumes most of one wall and looks onto a pebbled beach and an endless stretch of sea. In the distance, an elderly man hunts for mussels in the rocks, while at the table we dip into clotted cream, cranberry scones, raspberry cake, gingerbread, miniature loaves of bread, cookies, and strawberries. Annette chats about the difference between Cornish cream and Devon cream as I spread clotted cream onto her fluffy scones. "Oh, well done, dahling, look at that," she says to her husband, who is ascending the stairs with a newly baked baguette. In the distance a fishing boat drifts. Over sips of ruby-colored damson gin, I watch horses gallop along the shore. Soon in a haze of cookies, cream, and gin, the sound of Annette and Sue's banter blends with the wind chime.

Succumbing to a strange elixir of English high tea and jet lag, I soon find myself comfortably ensconced in the Citroën once again as we drift off onto another country road. The gentle zephyr of a coastal breeze meets my face and two hours pass before I know they are gone.

When I awake we are at Thornby Moor Dairy, where Caroline Fairbairn and her daughter Leonie are separating their curd from whey to make hard wheels of what will become well-aged goat cheese. Caroline has been making cheese from her own herd of goats for thirty years, Leonie for twenty-five years, since she was five years old. Leonie lives and breathes cheese. She is also a big Elvis fan and likes to listen to him while making deliveries in the British countryside. Gliding around the cheese room wearing black-and-white cow-patterned pants with knee-length rubber boots and an apron, Caroline is very busy. She wraps cylinders of goat's milk curd in cheesecloth and tops them with wooden "followers," round wooden blocks that help weigh them down and unify the curd. She fingers the long strands of hairy mold on small wheels as she describes her cheeses. Then she opens the door to the smokehouse, where dozens of bright orange wheels of oak-smoked Cumberland cheese are sitting on tar-covered racks.

Having spent the day driving up and down the northern reaches of England delivering butter, we arrive at our last stop, the home of one of Sue's customers who has run out of butter since the last monthly farmers' market. Sue restocks her customer with butter and a few quail eggs for good measure, which she retrieved from her neighbor.

During the course of the day, Sue has collected ingredients for "tea tonight"—potatoes, sausage, strawberries—from the various farms we have visited in Cumbria. Life seems to revolve around teatime. There is always time for tea.

Every day Sue sits down with her husband, daughter, son-in-law, and two grandsons for dinner. Tonight she serves the Cumberland sausage—a big spiral of pork patented for its secret spices. As we eat, I look out from the dinner table onto the barn studded with birdhouses. I had thought the requisite family dinner was something long lost in the imaginary world of 1950s television shows. At the very least this dinner is a reminder of the "ratchet effect" that has crept into modern life—of the successive generations of families who have acquired more and more things and debt along the way, and spent more and more hours at a desk, complicating their lives with the white noise of the modern world, and living less. Sue's grandfather lived to one hundred, her mother to ninety-five. Her family lives a life with a lot of silence and space in between the lines, a life in which they meet live turkeys at the train station and raise them for Christmas. The ratchet effect doesn't seem to have hit them—or at least it hasn't taken them away from the nightly dinner table.

After dinner Sue drives me along the Roman wall that divides Scotland from England. Her mother was born along this wall; the stone farm still stands, aged and worn, but with the unmistakable aura that there is nowhere else you'd rather be. Sue's father lived on a farm below her mother; he was one of twelve. The area was settled by Vikings, so a lot of their language was borrowed and it has settled into the words and dialect of the Cumbrians—"That yan owr there" ("that one over there").

In Cumbria it stays light for ages during the warmer months, and the day keeps going into the night. The sky is bigger, closer, more enveloping. The cows have not returned to their barns. Creamy yellow Charolais cows, long-haired Galloways, and meaty Belgian Blues recline on the grass ruminating.

The wall takes us past the dimly lit Naworth Castle where Lord Carlisle lives, then past the home of a bird-box maker, then past the old school that Sue attended as a child, and to Lanercost Priory, where she was christened. "It's a marvelous piece of engineering," she says of the wall. On either side of it, the fields are profoundly green, the sun brilliant with a disorienting evening light. We pass patches of butter burr, whose wide leaves were used before the days of refrigeration to keep butter cool. "And there's Peter Rabbit out having his tea," she says as a head of russet fur peers above a wide leaf.

It is ten by the time she drops me at the farmhouse where I am staying, and the sun is just setting.

The next morning, Dorothy, the farm owner, feeds me an English breakfast that includes a warm tomato. "We just be getting cattle ready for the auction mart," she says, appearing from behind a moving lorry full of cows as I leave. The lorry is making its way down the road. A wet, beige cow nose sticks out of the truck's grate as it moves away. I tell her that I am learning about Cumbrian butter, and she says, "That's grand." She says that a lot.

On my last morning with the Forresters, I am on my way back to Howberry to make butter. Along the narrow, wildflower lane the sour smell of manure thickens the crisp air and I am greeted by black-and-white Guinea hens.

In Sue's house everything carries the faint smell of room-temperature, slightly ripe cream. Once again, a large mixer is whirring slowly, whipping the double cream on its way to butter.

The color of the butter tells you what your cows have been eating. The butter at this time of year is very yellow and will be even brighter by the end of the summer as the cows eat more grass. If cows have been eating a lot of corn butter will be pale, though.

By the time we are done battering butter, I have a little pat for the road.

Sue's grandsons storm through the door as I leave. "Look, I found an egg, Grandma," Charlie says, revealing it from behind his back. As the boys' first real-live American visitor I am handed a crayon drawing of the farm and a very dirty duck egg as parting gifts.

With a pat of butter, a crayon drawing, and a stack of poems, I venture back through a tunnel of Queen Anne's Lace to pack up and to bid farewell to Dorothy. "Are you a farmer's daughter?" Dorothy asks as I leave.

"I'm working on it," I reply.

✿ BUTTER

As told to me in the farmhouse kitchen of Sue Forrester.

1. Find a farmer who will sell you raw milk. Depending on what state you live in, initially you may have to pick it up at the farm, but after not too long, I am willing to bet that a wink and a nod, or a secret handshake, will result in him passing it under the table at the farmers' market. Tell him you want to make butter and thus would like double cream. And if all else fails, buy heavy cream at the store.
2. Then slowly, in an electric mixer, churn the double cream until it separates into butterfat and buttermilk. The time will vary depending on the temperature, but it should take about 30 minutes.
3. Take out the butterfat with your hands and wash it thoroughly with water. Pour out the leftover buttermilk to use in scones (below) or to float in your coffee.
4. Separate the butterfat into desired portions. Using a paddle or your hands (but a paddle is more fun), shape it into blocks, add salt if you wish, and give it your special mark.

✿ BUTTERMILK SCONES

The future of your leftover buttermilk lies in these fluffy scones. Annette Gibbons shared her recipe with me right before she went to receive an O.B.E. award from the queen for her contributions to society. Short for "Officer in the Most Excellent Order of the Brisith Empire," it is one of the highest honors a civilian can obtain in Great Britain. Her scones alone are a lovely contribution to society. I have modified the recipe but it still tastes like Cumbria on a plate. Her recipes can be found in her book Home Grown in Cumbria and on her website, www.cumbriaonaplate.co.uk. Annette says, "I always use my hands and not a rolling pin to flatten the dough so that I'm being a bit more gentle with it and don't squash it too much. If you're baking at altitude, the oven temperature may need to be raised a bit, and use a little less baking powder."

Instead of prunes, you can add any other flavoring tidbits you desire: cooked and crumbled bacon, grated cheese, or any other dried fruit.

3 cups all-purpose flour
2½ teaspoons baking powder
1½ teaspoons powdered sugar
½ teaspoon salt
½ cup (1 stick) cold butter, cut into small pieces
½ cup prunes, coarsely chopped
About 1½ cup plain natural yogurt or buttermilk
1 large egg white, lightly beaten (optional)

1. Preheat the oven to 425°F.
2. Combine the flour, baking powder, powdered sugar, and salt in a large bowl. Rub the butter into the flour mixture with your fingers until it resembles fine sand. Toss in the prunes. Gradually stir in the yogurt, stirring until the dough just barely comes together. If you find you need more yogurt, add a teaspoon at a time so you don't overdo it.
3. Turn the dough out onto a floured board and press down gently. Lightly roll or use your fingers to flatten the dough to about ¾ inch thick. Using a ⅔-inch round cutter or an upside-down cup, stamp out scones and place them on a baking sheet. Brush the tops with egg white, if you'd like, for a shiny touch.
4. Bake for about 20 minutes, until golden brown. Eat immediately to enjoy them at their best, or let cool completely and freeze. To serve, thaw at room temperature and fill with fresh whipped double cream and thick strawberry jam.

MAKES ABOUT 10 SCONES

✿ LEMON CLOUDS CHEESECAKE

This recipe works best if, while you work, there is a five-year-old with thick glasses and a wild imagination talking to you in a Cumbrian accent. It doesn't require any baking and is very quick to prepare; it just needs time to set in the refrigerator.

> 1 (14.1-ounce) package digestive biscuits or graham crackers
> 8 tablespoons (1 stick) butter
> 1 (8-ounce) package cream cheese, at room temperature
> 1 cup lemon curd
> Juice of 2 lemons
> 2 cups heavy cream, whipped to soft peaks
> Lemon slices (optional)

1. Put the digestive biscuits in a sealed plastic bag and crush them with a rolling pin.
2. In a small saucepan, melt the butter; add the biscuit crumbs and stir to coat in the butter.
3. Press the mixture into the bottom and up the sides of a pie tin with the back of a spoon. The crust will still be crumbly, not uniform.
4. Whisk the cream cheese, lemon curd, and lemon juice together, then fold them into the whipped cream. Stick your finger in to see what lemon clouds taste like.
5. Pour the mixture into the pie tin and smooth the top with a knife. Garnish with lemon slices, if you'd like, and let it set in the refrigerator for at least 1 hour.

MAKES 1 LEMON CLOUD CHEESECAKE

STEVEN WALLACE

The Chocolate Entrepreneur

The Chocolate Pioneer

O n Greenwich Street in Manhattan, I am ruining the pristine, heart-shaped foam on top of my hot chocolate, swallowing mouthfuls with unbecoming speed. The drink is not cloying; it is thin and clear tasting—so distracting that I almost forget to tell him that I like it.

Steven Wallace is a rare entrepreneur. If he closes his eyes, he is transported back to Ghana, where, just a teen, he is awakened by roosters at daybreak. Through the window he can see the shirtless belly of the patriarch, Yao Brobbey, who is shaving in the courtyard of their compound. He is smiling, massaging his chubby flesh, looking at the new day with unclouded optimism. In Steven's mind he still walks the dirt roads of the village of Sunyani, following the good bread smells until he reaches a mud oven where his best friend Isaac and his mother are baking bread. On the way, children run over to him, yelling in Twi, "*Kwesi buroni!*" ("Good morning, sir!") and pressing their dark fingers into his tan skin, gleefully watching it blush pink.

It is 1978 and sixteen-year-old Steven Wallace has left his home in Wisconsin and moved to Ghana as an American Field Service exchange student. He lives in the village of Sunyani with a man, his three wives, and their twenty-one children. He has dysentery, the economy is terrible—and all he wants is a damned Coca-Cola.

On July 3, 1978—not long after he has stepped off the Swissair DC-10 at the Kotoka airport and onto sweltering Ghanaian tarmac, he experiences an awkward welcome. In a curious response to U.S. Independence Day, the existing military government of Ghana is over-thrown in a coup d'état. People are burned at the stake. Having grown up in the quintessential all-American town he describes as a throwback to the 1950s, Wallace realizes he is not in Wisconsin anymore.

"If I go back and read my journal, it was all I could do to keep it together. But then, that's when I fell in love with the country. 'A fish doesn't think about water until he's out of it,'" he says, quoting Robert Penn Warren. "It was time to consider who I was, the kind of person I wanted to become, and to reflect upon that elusive concept of what it might mean to be a citizen of the United States of America. It was time to get out of the water."

He learned that you don't know what a corrupt government is until you're truly living it—"It is jaw-dropping." But the people were so kind. His new house was a sort of compound, with an open middle where he ate outside over a fire every day. There were sleeping rooms outside the walls of the compound, where the children slept sometimes four to a bed. He had his own bed when no one else did. "I loved the place even though it was difficult. It was this complex percolation of emotions."

After three months Steven left Ghana, but, he says, "Ghana never left me." He spent the following years trying to find a way to go back with purpose. During and after college and then in law school, the memories lingered. But in the intervening years, he took the path of least resis-tance that was so often carved out for graduates of elite institutions. "Even though I was far from the top of my class, I had my choice of job offers and received a raise prior to even starting work because prospec-tive employers were so fearful of losing a recruit to a competing firm. A classmate quipped that we were like shrimp at a cocktail party—always in demand and never enough to go around."

He spent two years working at a tax boutique in Washington, D.C.—tax law because on some level he was simply a voyeur of wealth.

"Rich people hire tax lawyers, and I was curious about how the well-heeled lived and worked. It was not uncommon to be summoned to a client's home to sign wills and linger over a cup of Earl Grey on tufted sofas in living rooms lifted from Versailles while we tried to impress each other with pithy remarks." He was drawn to the clients more than to the other attorneys; he also craved a bit of the excitement they enjoyed while he could already clearly read the map of his life for the next thirty years: he envisioned decades of mastering the tax code, and it was scary. He wanted to accomplish something significant in his life, and it was apparent that it wasn't going to happen here. And so, at twenty-nine, he left his firm and set out to create the first company in the world to produce worldwide distribution of single-source chocolate—chocolate produced in the same country in which the cocoa beans used to make it are grown.

Ghana has vast cadres of bauxite, diamonds, gold, and cocoa. Lacking the expertise or money to establish aluminum smelters or gold mines, not quite prepared to go up against diamond cartels, Steve began to explore cocoa. "I had always enjoyed cooking, but had no formal training in food science. But I knew my way around a kitchen; it was big in my family. Well before any of the food TV shows, we would do little menus, pair wines with each course, we'd entertain and have fifty people over." He spent the evenings and weekends of the next two years researching cocoa and learned that Ghana grows what are considered the finest cocoa beans in the world. Yet Ghana struggles because the value of the country's cocoa exports is largely determined by the vagaries of world commodity markets, things like weather and crop parasites, which in turn affect the price farmers get for cocoa. When it got really bad, Ghanaian cocoa farmers would abandon their farms altogether.

He saw that Ghana was not producing finished chocolate for export; rather, it was exporting either raw cocoa beans or semiprocessed items to chocolatiers in the United States and Europe. These countries then added most of the value and earned the biggest margin by making the finished product themselves with a mixture of beans of various origins. Steve wanted to create a product whose selling price wasn't so closely linked to fluctuations in commodities prices and would also provide more stable wages for the workers and farmers.

"I had never sold a chocolate bar in my life. Not even as a Cub Scout," he says, cradling his second cup of hot chocolate. "But it hit me all at once. Chocolate bars. Why hadn't Ghana developed chocolate bars to successfully compete on the world market? Once I considered the idea of chocolate bars made in Ghana, I simply couldn't let go. Sure, Switzerland makes fine chocolate, but how many cacao trees actually grow in Zurich?"

So Steven Wallace got on a plane and went back to Ghana. He showed up and sat for hours in run-down offices dealing with illogical formalities and strict hierarchies, and requested meetings that were routinely denied. "Why don't you just tell him I'm here?" he'd ask, after six hours sitting and waiting in a tattered chair. "Well, you don't have an appointment," they'd say. "Well, I tried to get an appointment by phone, but your phones are down," he'd reply. "Oh, yes, we've had phone problems for two weeks. You'll have to come back," they'd say.

"They'd do anything not to deal with me," he recalls. "And then it made them uncomfortable. I'd go to Ghana and just sit there. It was humiliating. I'd sit for six hours in someone's office. My twins were thirteen months old, just beginning to walk. I had borrowed against all my life insurance. We should have been saving. I thought, What am I doing? There were times when I wanted to cry." Nothing happened for Steve Wallace for four years other than a lot of sitting and talking.

But then somehow it did. "I remember one man who worked for a division of the cocoa hierarchy; he called me and said, 'Can we just meet for a drink? I'd like to help you. How do we get this started?' Someone reached out their hand and said, 'Here's a way.'" Things began to move more quickly. Ghanaian government members found out he spoke a little Twi, and heard the story of his time in Sunyani, which gave him credibility. And because of his history in Sunyani, they checked on him, through a remarkably small network of people who all went to the same handful of schools. "I've never seen a country where with one phone call or one meeting in church they could check on you," he smiles. "And then they were intrigued. I wasn't asking for money. I was just trying to tell them this is what I want to do. I think stubbornness won them over. And then it became a point of pride. I got into it too deep, I couldn't not finish it, I wasn't just going away."

Fast-talking Americans had a history of coming into Ghana on Monday with big ideas and slick PowerPoint presentations, expecting to leave as millionaires on Friday. What Steve wanted to do was unprecedented: he wasn't asking for money, he was asking the government in Ghana to shift gears—all of the investment focus and development interest was on public works projects and large infrastructure installations, not small factory investments. Not only would this have to be Steve's money, but he had to structure it so that if it failed it was his fault, but if it worked it was everyone's success.

He began refurbishing part of a chocolate factory in a town called Tema between 1991 and 1994, which included planning, acquisition of capital goods, recipe development, label and package design, and finally actual production and export of chocolate. During those years he learned extreme patience and became ever more sensitive to cultural nuance. He observes, "You can't behave like a martinet and hope to win people over and have them enthusiastically adopt your vision. This is especially so when dealing in a cross-cultural context. I've seen red-faced consultants from Europe pounding on a table strewn with mechanical schematics, berating young Ghanaian engineers; the cause is lost. Public humiliation of your partners gets you nowhere fast in West Africa."

As he began experimenting with Ghanaian cocoa beans in his own kitchen, he saw the challenge was to produce a product entirely in Ghana that European and American markets would like and accept. As he toyed with the beans, he became convinced that it was possible. He describes it as a "combination of fear of failure, a healthy dose of naïveté, and a sort of stubbornness borne of a need to prove to myself and perhaps others that I knew what I was doing. Don't we all simply want to show the other kids on the playground that we aren't screw-ups?"

Today, in the very concentrated cacao-growing region of Ghana (20 percent of the country), just south of the midpoint, a Ghanaian farmer plucks a ripe cocoa pod the size of a Nerf football from a cacao tree as small as an apple tree. Inside the pod are two dozen cocoa beans covered in white film. You can suck on them—they are saccharin sweet, but they don't taste like cocoa. The farmer puts the beans between two interwoven banana leaves and places them on the rainforest floor. For ten to fourteen days the leaves are flipped back and forth. As the beans dry in the sun, they ferment slightly and the film starts to slough off, slowly reducing the moisture content, concentrating the sugars, enhancing the flavor. The farmer transfers them to bamboo mats, where they are sun-dried and turn a wonderful chocolate color. The fermented beans soon arrive at the Omanhene chocolate factory in Tema. Steve chose the name Omanhene ("OH-man-HEE-nee") as a reflection of the culture he was so familiar with: in Twi it means "paramount chief," the pillar figure of every Ghanaian community, the repository of ethical and moral authority.

His factory workers are among the highest paid in the country. They are unionized and are equity shareholders in the company. They receive free uniforms, subsidized housing, free meals, free transportation to and from work, and free medical care for themselves and their families. Once they get picked up from their houses and don their white jumpsuits, they set to work on a specific task, roasting the raw beans until the factory wells with divine odor; then kibbling it into little pebbles called "nibs," then crushing the nibs with heated pressure until they liquefy at the bottom of a vat into a dark brown, almost black cocoa liquor. This liquor contains the three hundred chemical compounds that give chocolate its elusive and addictive quality. What floats to the top of the liquor is the clear, odorless, flavorless liquid called cocoa butter that gives chocolate that special feel in the mouth.

After half a day of making chocolate, all three hundred Ghanaian employees break for lunch and sing a cappella in a community choir they have formed. "I think it is considered a wonderful place to work," Steve says thoughtfully. "What we're trying to do is significant." Despite being part of an economy that gets 44 to 50 percent of its GDP from cocoa export, many of Steve's Ghanaian workers had never before tasted chocolate in this form.

His particular chocolate has a very simple ingredients list: cocoa liquor, the butter, sugar, and soy lecithin (the latter added so that the liquor and cocoa butter don't separate). Some people add vanilla to their chocolate, some give their chocolate a "bicarbonate bath" to reduce the bitterness, but he decided early on "love it or leave it. We're going to make natural chocolate. What you're going to get is like a single-malt Scotch, or an estate-bottled wine. It is from the earth, from the *terroir*." Omanhene soon not only became the first single-origin chocolate, and the first to manufacture entirely in the country, but also introduced the first dark milk chocolate to the world—a milk chocolate bar with a very high percentage of cocoa liquor. This percentage is often expressed as being of cocoa solids (the combination of cocoa liquor and cocoa butter, sometimes called cocoa mass), however cocoa liquor is the only component that adds flavor and aroma to the chocolate bar and it the only number that should interest consumers who want to find out which chocolate bar is "darkest." Cocoa butter simply provides the "mouthfeel." Few chocolatiers will reveal the exact percentages of butter and liquor in their recipes and prefer to hide behind the cocoa solids "combined" number. Unless you know what percentage of the total cocoa solids percentage is actually cocoa liquor, you don't know which is the "darker" more flavorful chocolate.

In this Manhattan café, he opens small glass vials of cocoa in their various stages and I sniff the raw cocoa beans; they smell like sour feet. Then the roasted ones, which smell nuttier and better; then the nibs, better still; then the crushed powder, and in that aroma I can taste the chocolate. Next I smell the alcoholic singe of cocoa liquor, and then he hands me the chocolate. "Open it up and snap it between your thumb and forefinger," he says. "It will snap. Good chocolate should melt on your hands. Hold it on your tongue. Keep it on the roof of your mouth. You are waiting for the sharp edges to soften." I obey with careful precision and experience the tang and mystery of the aftertaste, a currant or a sharp raspberry. "That's from a really fresh bean," he says, reading my smile. "Our beans aren't fumigated, they're not put in the hold of a ship, subjected to a six-week voyage by sea, and then turned into chocolate." That is what robs chocolate of its magic, takes away this special freshness and buoyancy. "Ghana is blessed with great soil, a great climate, and now these great techniques. No one else does the fermenting, and sun-drying. You can do it in a factory and mechanically dry it, but you don't get the same effect."

———————

Ghana as a country is a pioneer, too, though the story is rarely told. When world commodities prices fell, the government found a way to help their farmers in the early 1960s. By setting up a series of government monopolies, they began guaranteeing their farmers a price for their cocoa beans. The government began controlling the distribution of seeds, which farmers could then sell back to the government at the end of the season. If the world price went above what they were paid, the farmers got a bonus; if it went below, they were protected. It is a series of vertically integrated bureaucracies that control cocoa marketing, cocoa distribution, and cocoa procurement. From an outsider's perspective the idea of state-owned enterprises seems like an alarming throwback to communism in the Soviet Union. But here, quietly, it seems to work. Even the United Nations has acknowledged that Ghana is an exception because they have actually managed to get a higher price for their farmers and also prevent foreign business from negotiating with cocoa farmers directly—farmers who don't have market knowledge and could easily be exploited. With almost 700,000 individual cocoa farms, roughly 9 million people, which translate into 9 million votes (Ghana is in its twelfth year of democratic elections), the cocoa farmers are now the wealthiest class in Ghana. It is a hard life (there isn't running water on some farms, for example), but the wealth that it can create for a farmer is not insignificant, and it supports a lot of people.

Amid all of these levels of enterprise—from the bean buying, grading, and sorting, to the selling and first-stage processing, to the cocoa board, the finance ministry, and bank of Ghana—Steve Wallace has inserted his little chocolate-bar company into the vertical monopoly. And he did it by slowly building a relationship of trust with the people of Ghana over the course of thirty-one years, from the time he was a sixteen-year-old boy transplanted to the village of Sunyani.

"War and disease are what people associate with Africa. I think it is important to dispel these kind of notions. I wanted this to be sustainable, so I didn't want to be charitable. That stigma is paternalistic. My job is changing the perception. There is a culinary, human potential in Ghana's culture. People can now start to say, 'Oh, I know Ghana—that's where that cocoa comes from.'" So Steve is dreaming big. One day he wants to build a restaurant and culinary school so that chefs don't have to be imported from Europe, and Ghana can showcase its own talent; he wants to create a more intensive experience, train chefs, educate them in how to run a restaurant financially.

"Everyone is concerned with pennies, everyone wants to get more pennies for the farmers. That is my critique of the fair-trade movement. I want to get away from that and give people in Ghana the real skills to do it themselves." He dreams of a day when not a single bean leaves Ghana, where every cocoa bean is processed into something, so that the money stays within the country's economy. He thinks the steps Ghana has already taken to help itself are a brilliant solution. "People say, 'Isn't all of that vertical monopoly frustrating?' Yes, but it plays a role in quality. It is a huge story."

Writers who visit Africa are looking for the exposé, the child slavery angle, the dramatic and the horrific—success stories don't sell. The Ghanaian government is conscious of that, and it makes them wary, particularly of visiting writers. They don't want to be compared to the Ivory Coast, which does have large corporate cocoa farms powered by slave labor, where the average farm size is four hundred acres (in Ghana the largest is forty acres), where the political history of colonization by the French is very different from Ghana's, which was colonized by the British.

Whereas Ghana monitors family farms to prevent child labor and to ensure school attendance, the Ivory Coast has for years had a more corrupt government: big commodity processors like Cargill, ABM, and Barry Callebaut offered million-dollar factory investments (with government kickbacks) in exchange for cheap beans at 30 to 40 percent less than the world price. To get cocoa that cheap, you have to disenfranchise the workers, take them off their family farms, and put them in corporate farms. You have to have a cheap, mobile labor force that can easily be transported from Mali to the Ivory Coast to work on these big farms. In Ghana, by contrast, there is a prevailing sense of brotherhood among the workers, and pride in the product of their labor.

A day in the life of a cocoa worker is very different at Omanhene than it is at a Cargill operation. But what hasn't changed is the attitude of the U.S. consumer who, strolling down the packed aisles of Whole Foods, will make a choice between a beautifully packaged chocolate bar from a Swiss company that bought its beans from many sources and an African chocolate bar called Omanhene, a name they probably can't pronounce. Most will opt for the familiar, paying the sticker price, unaware of the implications of their choice.

"I try to be even-keeled when negotiating business transactions," Steve says, "but it would be incorrect to say that I'm not emotional—to the contrary. I still get excited by the smallest moments. I was in a store and this woman was in a hurry—wearing biking shorts, a Livestrong wristband, and a Dave Matthews T-shirt. And she was holding two items: a quart of strawberries and a container of our hot cocoa mix. And I could have just jumped the aisle and hugged her and said, 'Thank you! What are you doing with this?' It was such a remarkable thing right there in the checkout aisle, and I thought, this is why I do it. This is the miracle of business that I wish I could share with everyone. It worked, it's out there. Of the two items this woman wanted for some special occasion, we were one." He wonders if the CEOs of the established businesses and multinationals ever want to hug a customer. He wonders if they ever feel the same range of emotions, or whether it ever gets that personal for them.

But Steve embraces the emotional ride that comes with being an entrepreneur. It makes the journey more meaningful. "Often, talk of entrepreneurship devolves into a series of neat aphorisms from Sun-Tzu's *Art of War* to Machiavelli's *The Prince*. I believe the measure of success is marked by the emotional commitment made, and emotionalism is the antithesis of intellect—indeed, the measure of emotional commitment needs to be strongest when all objective benchmarks tell you to quit. It is something that cuts right to the very heart of the matter. And it just might be the best predictor of entrepreneurial success."

Steve still sees Yao Brobbey, the patriarch of Sunyani. He lost track of him for a decade, and when he saw him again, Brobbey's rotund body was emaciated and he was missing teeth. He had been jailed for five years for having a half interest in a Ford tractor that he could lease out to other farmers, and for having a little kiosk without anything on the shelves to sell, and for farming cassava—in other words, for being an entrepreneur. He still smiles all the time, and is still sweet, still has a Santa Claus demeanor despite the tumult. He has become Catholic, married just one of his wives, and has restored his house. He kept his little entrepreneurial flame going, undercover, and in this he shares something with Steve.

"I look back on it," Steve says, leaning back on a pleather sofa and sipping his hot chocolate, "and it happened over the course of years. It's funny, maybe because it weighs on you with the passage of time. Having worked with the junior people who are now running things, there's a comfort level of having worked with them. Thirty-one years of being in the country. It has taken years to sort of process."

I walk the streets of New York with Steve, participating in a few fleeting moments of his thirty-one-year odyssey, seeing his box of chocolate tucked protectively under his arm, watching him look up at the buildings with a schoolboy's optimism and man-on-a-mission air. "Is it better than being a tax attorney?" he laughs. "Yes, but maybe I wasn't that good a tax attorney."

"This is a life's work and probably then some. It's such a fun journey. It's everything I wanted. I'll go back to reunions on occasions. Everyone is partner now at their firms. And they've fulfilled everything they wanted to do since law school. And still they all want to do what I'm doing. I don't know that I could take over someone else's chocolate company and run it. I kind of like building the castle from the ground up more than running it. We're going to persevere, be the little chocolate company that could."

✍ HOT HOT CHOCOLATE

The Aztec chocolate drink was bitter, frothy, and spicy. It was often seasoned with vanilla and chiles, and was believed to fight fatigue. This is a sweet and spicy version of the drink. You can reduce the amount of cayenne to suit your taste.

> 2 cups milk
> 6 ½ ounces good-quality semisweet or bittersweet dark chocolate, chopped (about ¾ cup)
> ¼ teaspoon ground cayenne
> ¼ teaspoon ground cinnamon
> Crème fraîche, mascarpone, or whipped cream (optional)

1. Put the milk and chocolate in a medium saucepan over medium heat and whisk until the mixture reaches the boiling point and is foamy. Sprinkle in the cayenne and cinnamon and whisk to combine.
2. Remove from the heat and, if you wish, add a dollop of crème fraîche.

MAKES ABOUT 2 CUPS OF HOT HOT CHOCOLATE

FRENCH CHOCOLATE CHIP COOKIES

Adapted from my days in France.

I experienced these cookies for the first time when a restaurant manager, Michelle, picked me up from the train station in Provence and sat me down in the dining room looking out through the open doors to the garden. He poured me wine and sent me amazing food until I had to stop him. But just for good measure he took me into the kitchen and made me try a warm cookie. The secret to these cookies is the raw sugar, which gives them a crunchy texture. And there is far less sugar than in most cookies, which allows you to taste all of the other flavors.

1 ¾ cups (3 ½ sticks) butter
1 ½ cups raw sugar
½ teaspoon salt
3 ½ cups all-purpose flour
2 large eggs
1 ½ cups walnuts or pecans, roughly chopped
2 cups dark chocolate pieces, roughly chopped

1. Preheat the oven to 400°F.
2. Generously grease a baking sheet.
3. With an electric mixer fitted with the paddle attachment, beat the butter, sugar, and salt together until fluffy. With the mixer on low speed, add the flour, then the eggs. Add the nuts and chocolate and mix until just combined.
4. Drop heaping spoonfuls of the mixture onto the baking sheet about 2 inches apart. Bake for 15 minutes, or until the edges are golden brown. Remove to wire racks and let cool. These cookies will be chunky and chewy, with lots of texture.

Note: You can make extra cookie dough and roll it into thick, long logs. Wrap the logs in plastic wrap and then in aluminum foil and freeze them. When you are ready for a warm cookie, slice 1-inch rounds from the log and bake them as needed.

MAKES ABOUT 2 DOZEN FRENCH COOKIES

RHODA ADAMS

The Tamale Queen

Sanctified Tamales

"Hot Fried Catfish" signs mingle with shiny silver silos on the journey through the Arkansas Delta, past orange fields of corn and cotton that go and go. Bodies of abandoned trucks lie across patches of dehydrated grass, alternating with a Baptist church every few miles. The swampy air captures the dust floating above the dirt roads, the aftermath of lone cars, and turns into an iridescent haze. This place, this vast stretch of land sprinkled with tired signs and the placid sight of things growing, feels like the end of the earth. It is a peaceful place full of quiet, where people go when they need to be let alone, when they need peace.

And it is where they go when they need coconut and chocolate and lemon cream pies, or the high flavor of roasting pig, or the reassuring feeling of a hot tamale weighing in their bellies.

No one really knows exactly where this place, the Delta, starts. It is a mindset, a way of life, more than a geographic boundary. It traces the contours of the southern states along the Mexican Gulf. But to the people of this region, it really begins when the mosquitoes approach the size of butterflies and ends 350 miles north in the lobby of the Peabody

Hotel in Memphis. It is a culture of hard drink and cultivated cuisine born from a lack of much else, and an acute connection to the land.

On Saint Mary Street in Lake Village, Arkansas, is a white shack with a floor of uneven wood and walls banked with metal spoons of many sizes. Inside is Rhoda Adams, sitting in a chair over a bowl of oatmeal, her feet resting above her slip-ons.

"Y'all come back!" she says as two of her customers exit and the doorbells chime. Here, Rhoda has been making hot tamales for "thirty-something years." For Rhoda it was a calling, not a way of life she ever planned. "I never wanted to start," she says, as matter of fact as it can be. "I was selling cupcakes and different stuff for the church. And they told us to start making pies, and I'd never made but one pie." She leans back against the wall; an episode of *All My Children*, glows from the television hanging on the wall. The high-pitched noises of synthesized violins flow in and out of the room, gay, melancholy, falsely mysterious.

"I said, I'm going to do what the Lord told me to do. So I did what the Lord told me to do. I would go around and sell cupcakes and popcorn and I was workin' hard out of my house for the church. And hon, I had eleven heads of children. And I asked the church if they'd help me. And nobody really helped me. A woman in the church said, 'Go in business for yourself.' And I said, 'The Lord told me to do it for the church. I don't want to do it for me.' And she said, 'Well, there ain't nobody to help you.' So I waited for a few months. And hon, this place is so busy."

The fumes from a simmering pot cross the room, the air redolent with chicken fat, meal, and spice. James Adams, Rhoda's husband, is patiently ladling tamale juice from one pot to the next, the orange corn-husk packages emitting a pretty, eternal ooze.

Rhoda gets up and begins to fill pie crusts with flavored creams, yellow, white, and brown. "I had some made, but my husband sold them all," she says, making a splattering sound with each dollop she drops into a baked shell. Pecan pies and sweet potato pies line the counter too, some with two flavors filling one crust, a half moon for each flavor.

Jackie, their granddaughter, works dough on a well-used cutting board, her hair slung up in a red bandana. Rhoda spoons applesauce onto circles of dough, then folds them and presses the edges with a fork, then drops them in hot oil. These are her fried pies. Lifting a pie, crisp and dripping from the oil, she says, "A man come in here and said he wanted some of Rhoda's fried pies for his wedding cakes. We got him some fried pies for the wedding."

James begins to transfer little corn husks tied in bunches of three into another metal pot. These are her famous tamales—a mix of corn, pork, beef, and chicken thighs, skin on. People say there is something special about her tamales, something different. Maybe it has to do with the fact that she spends half her time cooking and the other half praying. Salvation is in these tamales.

This ancient food, with roots in Latin America, has had a presence in Arkansas since at least the turn of the twentieth century. No one is quite sure how tamales made their way to the Delta, or why, so popular here, they haven't spread beyond the region. Some think they came with the soldiers returning from the Mexican War, others think it is Native American influence, most think they were introduced by Latino migrant workers who worked the cotton fields along the Mississippi River. Tamales were made of familiar ingredients, portable bundles of coarse-textured meat and meal, a practical, warm, filling lunch in the wet, hot fields. Once sold out of people's homes, now sold out of roadside shacks, they are filled with pork and corn, bedrock ingredients of traditional Deep South cooking.

I watch the lean hands of James Adams move among rolling pins, metal pots, and dented ladles, stirring, tying, and pouring a red juice that steams and tastes like delicious meal in my throat. "There's pepper and different stuff in there, you know," he informs me. "We got to spice it up for 'em." His face is bent keen and intent above the tamales.

Rhoda shares her secret, eyes wide and candid. "Take your time and do 'em right and cook 'em with love. People come in here and say, 'Rhoda you've got a lot of love.'"

I unwrap a damp husk, warm as love, and dab at the insides with a saltine. Utensils have never been part of tamale technique. It is mildly potent, quietly sustaining, comforting like hot buttered toast or the smell of a fire burning. Cayenne and chicken juice cover my tongue.

Rhoda sits down again to take a rest and eat a chili cheeseburger. She works every day but Sunday. She says, "People call here on Sunday and say, 'Rhoda, are you open? I want some *hot* tamales.'" The emphases on her words are like undulating waves that throw you off balance.

Then turning, she cries out, "How y'all doin?" to a trio of incoming patrons. "I got hot tamales, and hamburgers, and cheeseburgers, and pies. Now whatchu want?"

"I want soul food," the man replies with a grin.

She laughs. "Man, they workin' so hard. Now, I have some spaghetti. I can put some sauce on it and cook y'all some fish."

"He'd love some fish," the man's lady friend replies.

"You got fish? I'll take some fish," he says.

"Is he worth it?" Rhoda asks the woman.

"Yeah, he's worth it."

"Hon, let's throw on some fish. Now you sit down."

James is sitting on his stool, carefully making square burgers on the Formica. With his fingertips he presses hearty potions of raw meat against squares of parchment. "People like them square burgers. We try to give people their money's worth." Then he says, "Always pray before something happens; it's too late to pray when it happens." He begins to spank the burgers. "Ever been to Vegas?" he asks. "Gotta keep this up so we can go visit our daughter in Vegas." He and Rhoda have been married for fifty-six years. "I couldn't tell you how many grandchildren we have!" Then he murmurs something about there being great-grandchildren and great-great-grandchildren in the mix.

"You wanna taste mine?" Rhoda asks, bringing over her chili cheeseburger. She cuts me a neat little piece like it is a pie.

"That's a Rhoda burger," James says. "I don't mind being in a book but I want people to see you for your fancy work. Really, I want to have a sign made. Maybe one with lights and my wife's picture on it." Then he rolls over his square burgers with a rolling pin. Slowly, evenly, carefully, just so.

One of the customers, now sitting under the humming TV, requests her burger onions well grilled. "You see this burger right here?" Rhoda says. "That's got grilled onions on it." The woman supposes she will need gum afterward. "You act like I ain't got no gum. Baby, this is a store." Rhoda laughs heavily.

The threesome soon bow their heads and mutter their prayers in unison over their plates of tamales. Sometimes, if you catch her in a spiritual moment, Rhoda will pray over your tamales with you, and they will become "sanctified tamales."

She sells them by the dozen: three dozen come in a coffee can for $29.97 cash. Her customers come from near and far, and among the most extreme is a man who flies his jet in once a month for his supply. But on any given afternoon you will hear a customer mention that he or she has driven seven hours or thereabouts to visit Rhoda. She greets them calmly from the same chair, her silvering hair often pasted in a spiral around her head.

Hunters and anglers arrive, too, in their Silverados and Tahoes, wearing their seasonal outfits of camouflage, the hunters still with orange plugs in their ears, after a morning of daybreak dove hunting or crappie catching.

Rhoda greets them: "Hey! Whatch'all want?"

And most often they reply, "A dozen hot tamales."

And always she will reply with some snappy version of, "I know that ain't all." Then she will smile and laugh. And as she laughs the light will twinkle off the gold rim of her left tooth.

By now the threesome has moved on to miniature pecan pies, and Jackie is snacking from a tray full of beautiful little cupcakes, each the size of one lavish bite. James begins loading the maroon van with metal pots of tamales, cream pies, and candy sticks so that Rhoda can take her "fancy work" down the road to sell (and pray), in front of a popular store.

She smiles and waves while I snap pictures of her. "I got my hair permed and all wrapped up around my head. I said I was gonna keep it that way till tomorrow. I don't know how it's gonna look on camera. Lord have mercy."

She slides herself into the driver's seat. "Thank you, baby," she says and begins buzzing down the highway. I wonder what chord it is in my nature that vibrates at this sight. It represents vanished days, full of the traditional bits of nourishment I seek.

✒ TAMALES

The food Rhoda cooks is the kind that brings people together; the kind that makes you want to sit at a table for hours and laugh and eat and laugh some more, well into the night as lunch becomes dinner and dinner becomes a warm snack.

This is a recipe that requires dedication. But it pays dividends—in tamales—for many months afterward, as you pluck them from your freezer and reap the reward. The process from beginning to end will take roughly 5 hours, but will go more quickly with the help of many hands.

> 1 (4-pound) pork roast
> 1 (4-pound) beef roast
> 1 (5-pound) chicken
> 2 ½ cups olive oil
> 6 tablespoons garlic powder
> 3 tablespoons ground cumin
> 9 tablespoons chili powder
> 8 cups masa harina
> 3 tablespoons paprika
> 1 tablespoon cumin seeds
> Corn husks, soaked in warm water for 2 hours (see Note)
> Salt and black pepper

1. Preheat the oven to 400°F.
2. Cut the roasts into large chunks, each about the size of a fist. Put them in a roasting pan and add enough water to halfway cover the meat. Cover the pan with aluminum foil and roast until very tender, about 2 hours. Let the meat cool in the liquid. Reserve the liquid and shred the meat thoroughly, removing any fat and cartilage along the way. Meanwhile, put the chicken in a large pot and cover completely with water. Boil for about 2 hours. Reserve the liquid and remove the skin and bones from the chicken, shredding the meat.

3. In a large bowl, combine all of the meat with ½ cup of the oil, 3 tablespoons of the garlic powder, the ground cumin, 6 tablespoons of the chili powder, 2 tablespoons salt, and 1 tablespoon black pepper. Work the mixture until completely uniform.

4. In another large bowl, combine the masa harina with the paprika, cumin seeds, the remaining 3 tablespoons chili powder, the remaining 3 tablespoons garlic powder, and 3 tablespoons salt. Mix thoroughly.

5. Combine the warm broth from the chicken and roasts and skim off all the fat. Add the remaining 2 cups oil to the masa mixture, then gradually ladle in 8 cups of the broth, mixing well as you go, until the consistency is like that of thick peanut butter.

6. Remove the softened corn husks from the water, dry them well, and place them on a work surface. Spread about ½ cup of the masa paste on the inside of the husk, making sure to leave space on the tapered side of the husk so you can fold it later. Put about 2 tablespoons of the shredded meat mixture on top of the masa paste. Roll the tamale husk so it looks like a tube, and fold the tapered edge over like an envelope.

7. Place all of the tamales, open end up, in a large steamer, tightly packed so they don't unfold while they cook. Pour 6 cups water into the steamer. Cover the pot and steam for 2 hours over low heat, adding more water if needed. To check doneness, open a tamale up to see if the masa is cooked through.

8. Serve immediately or let cool completely and freeze.

Note: Corn husks can be purchased at good supermarkets, in Mexican grocery stores, or online.

MAKES 4 DOZEN TAMALES

BANANAS FOSTER CUPCAKES

Bananas Foster is a French Creole dessert invented in New Orleans. It features bananas flambéed with rum and vanilla. These cupcakes are inspired by this classic Delta dessert and by the mounds of cream in Rhoda's store.

For the cupcakes:
    1½ cups all-purpose or cake flour
    1 teaspoon baking powder
    ½ teaspoon salt
    ¾ cup (1½ sticks) butter, at room temperature
    ⅓ plus 2 tablespoons sugar
    1 ripe banana, pureed
    ½ teaspoon rum
    ½ cup coconut milk
    4 large egg whites

For the cream filling:
    ¾ cup sugar
    ½ cup all-purpose flour
    ½ teaspoon salt
    4 large egg yolks
    1½ cups coconut milk
    1 teaspoon rum
    1 tablespoon butter

For the icing:
    ¾ cup sugar
    Pinch of salt
    2 tablespoons coconut milk
    ¼ teaspoon cream of tartar
    2 large egg whites
    1 teaspoon rum

1.   Make the cupcakes: Preheat the oven to 350°F. Line a standard muffin pan with paper liners or butter the cups.

2. In a large bowl, whisk together the flour, baking powder, and salt and set aside. With an electric mixer fitted with the paddle attachment, beat the butter and ⅓ cup of the sugar together until light and fluffy, 3 to 4 minutes, scraping down the sides of the bowl as needed. Beat in the banana and then the rum. With the mixer on low speed, add the flour mixture in three parts, alternating with the coconut milk, until just combined. Transfer the mixture to a large bowl and set aside.

3. Rinse the mixing bowl. Using the whisk attachment, beat the egg whites on low speed until foamy. With the mixer running, gradually add the remaining 2 tablespoons sugar and beat on high speed until stiff, glossy peaks form, about 4 minutes. Don't overbeat, or they will turn lumpy. Gently fold one-third of the egg-white mixture into the butter-flour mixture until combined. Gently fold in the rest.

4. Divide the batter evenly among the muffin cups. Bake, rotating the pan halfway through the baking time, until the cupcakes are golden brown and a toothpick inserted in the center of a cupcake comes out clean, 25 to 30 minutes. Let cool completely.

5. Make the cream filling: Combine the sugar, flour, and salt in a bowl, and stir well to mix so there are no lumps. Set aside.

6. In a heavy saucepan, beat the egg yolks well with a whisk. Over low heat, add the flour mixture, alternating with the coconut milk and rum, stirring constantly with a wooden spoon and scraping the sides and corners of the saucepan as you go so the egg doesn't scramble. When the mixture begins to thicken, add the butter, continuing to stir. Keep stirring until the mixture reaches a nice pudding consistency, about 10 minutes. Remove from the heat.

7. Fit a pastry bag with a small tip and fill it with the cream. Push the tip through the bottom of each cupcake and gently squeeze the pudding into the middle.

8. Make the icing: Combine all of the ingredients except the rum in the top of a double boiler over simmering water and whisk constantly until it becomes thick and glossy, about 7 minutes, adding the rum halfway through. Let it cool a bit, then spoon pillowy mounds of it on top of each cupcake.

MAKES 1 DOZEN LAVISH CUPCAKES

TOSH KURATOMI

The Persimmon Grower

The Persimmon Masseuse

O n a verdant hill in Granite Bay, California, Helen Otow sits in a wooden chair in her driveway. She is ninety-three, thin and frail, her puckered face at odds with the slick aviator sunglasses she wears. Intently, she leans into the task at hand, her delicate fingers gently rubbing, working, and molding the skins of one persimmon at a time. They hang like little golden jack-o'-lanterns, swaying in the wind, tied to the white threads she has carefully fastened to each stem. A north wind rocks them back and forth. They begin to glow, translucent in the light, the white powder on their flesh like broken glass glittering in the sun. As the wind slaps her face, she remains still, never changing her long fixed expression. She doesn't speak, doesn't return a smile, just continues to massage, the same way she always has, the same way she watched her mother do it as a child.

Mrs. Otow specializes in the ancient art of *hoshigaki*, hand-massaged dried persimmons. It requires patience, careful monitoring, and dexterity. It is slow and laborious, making it economically unfeasible for all but the most passionate practitioners of the art. I crouch down by the dirt driveway, a distance from her, and timidly take one between my fingers. It feels like a small water balloon, the leathered skin taut around the pulpy inside.

From October to December, persimmons are plucked from the trees, peeled, and hung, one on either end of a string. They dry and dangle over wooden slats in the sun, swaying to and fro where the wind blows strong. They are turned by hand over and over again so they dry uniformly. After a week has passed, they collapse, and become soft. Each persimmon is then hand massaged every three to five days for three to five weeks until the hard inner pulp is dissolved and you can no longer roll it in your hands. In the end, the sugar comes to the surface of the wrinkled skins, a white bloom of glaze.

These soft dried persimmons are a delicacy in Japan. But the art of *hoshigaki* is dying even there. The Hachiya persimmon is traditionally used while still hard, because of its high tannic content and astringent taste that, when dried, becomes sweet and soft. It is a variety native to the village of Hachiyamachi, in the Minokamo Gifu prefecture, near the town of Minokamo. There the winters are particularly mild. This village once offered *hoshigaki* to the imperial court in the middle of the Heian period, from 794 A.D. to 1185 A.D., and received special privileges in return. After hundreds of years, reform took place, modern industry took over, and persimmon fields were slowly replaced with more profitable exports.

But during the Showa period, in the 1940s, a young Japanese farmer named Toshio Murase embarked on a quest to revive the tradition of *hoshigaki*. He discovered an original mother tree in the garden of an old house, and despite government orders to increase other food production in wartime, he kept the tradition alive with the help of old villagers. Years later, in 1978, he founded an association to promote *hoshigaki*. The mother tree is now protected and used to obtain grafts that are distributed to other members of the association so it can be passed down for generations. The association holds an annual course for young children to learn the craft, and the product is distributed to old villagers in Hachiyamachi.

As the ancient practice struggles in Japan, it hangs on by a thread in America, still practiced by a few Japanese-American farmers whose ancestors brought it with them. It is inextricably tied to the Japanese community in Placer County, California, a kind of Hachiyamachi of the United States, but has all but disappeared from commercial production. Except in this place where I stand, watching Mrs. Otow gently massage her persimmons. Here a small commercial operation continues, carried on by her daughter Chris Otow Kuratomi and son-in-law Tosh Kuratomi. It is a family business that began when Chris's grandparents immigrated to northern California in the late 1800s.

～～～

Tosh Kuratomi appears from around the corner, rolling a stack of wooden boxes filled with apples from a farmer on the hill. His chin-length silver hair is tucked under a baseball hat, and he carries the sound of a smile in his voice as he invites me to the persimmon orchard. We walk among the fruit trees, blazing orange. There are eight varieties dangling above our heads. He pulls them down, some spotted black with sunburn, and offers them. "You can take a bite of that one if you want it," he says. "It will be like a tomato."

I bite the fruit in my hand and swallow all the soft flesh and skin. "It is nature's pudding," he smiles, the sun reflecting off his teeth. "My grandfather used to send me boxes of these persimmons while I was in college."

Tosh's ancestors, like many Japanese Americans before World War II, were congregated in California: his father had a store in San Diego, and his mother worked in San Francisco. But in the wake of Japan's attack on Pearl Harbor, they were among the many thrown into American internment camps. In order to be released, they had to go to school, or had to be promised a job elsewhere, so many families dispersed. "My in-laws went to Chicago and then came back after the war," he says, plucking more persimmons. "People were generally evacuated and moved by region. Then as the war progressed they had to forswear their allegiance to the emperor of Japan. So some people protested. They said, 'We're Americans—what allegiance do we have? If we mark "yes" that means we were loyal to the emperor before.' And so they refused to sign. And the other question was, 'Will you serve in the military if asked to?' And some people were just openly hostile to that because here they were in prison and were not about to turn around and say 'Sure, we'll go die in a war.' So they started isolating or segregating these people in the different camps." That is how his parents met, in an American internment camp.

He plucks a giant Fuyu persimmon and turns it in his palm. "Fruit is always supposed to have that white bloom on it," he says, rubbing it with his shirtsleeve. "People polish them up so they look pretty, but they should have that bloom to indicate they are fresh. And it's very difficult to know if they're going to be chocolate or not," he adds. The Fuyu, when pollinated, is a chocolate color inside, sweet, and a little more round. When it is not pollinated, it is white inside and tart. "They are usually very hard; people don't like them. But unless we can market some of them as heritage, we're going to lose some of these things, they're going to be gone."

As we walk past one hundred white beehives he tells me that his own path to the practice of making *hoshigaki* was a winding one. He was in the military in the 1960s, stationed in Guam. "It was exciting to see people from around the world working on the island, teaching school, building hospitals. But then my grandmother died, and my grandfather, who was in his eighties, was living by himself. So I got transferred back, went to graduate school, got married . . . My grandfather used to dry persimmons, but his were always hard as a rock. My mother-in-law wouldn't sell them because they were too hard. Others were too soft and she was worried about mold." In their retirement, Tosh and Chris have taken over much of the work on Mrs. Otow's farm, in order to keep the tradition alive. They try their own methods, which Tosh admits are too crude, not systematic enough for Mrs. Otow. "She's very orderly," he says with a chuckle.

We arrive at a truck parked in the orchard between a row of plum trees and a row of apricots. He tries to start it. "I think what it is, is it's out of gas," he says calmly. He doesn't have a fastidious way about him; he lets things unfold as they are meant to. He plants his fruit trees in random order and lets nature make decisions for herself. He inserts himself only where it is essential.

We walk toward the farm sheds, past a jujube tree dangling with walnut-size, glossy red Chinese dates, a tree he bought because he remembers his ancestors having them. As we go, we step over lustrous soft fallen fruit, which he leaves on the ground because he doesn't want the liability. "We have probably gotten to be a little too clean in our society where we don't have enough exposure to bacteria, so we're not as immune to it," he says. We pass an adobe oven and stop across from Mrs. Otow and her glowing jack-o'-lanterns. In a small room, a South American woman named Veronica peels persimmons with her newborn cooing by her side. Veronica's husband helps pick them in the fields. It is not enough help, but it works.

Tosh shows me how to peel persimmons as Mocha, the beagle, catches the scraps falling to our feet. He slips the knife under the stem and trims off the edge of the calyx. Then with a peeler, he pulls down vertically along the contours of the flesh, pulls off any nicks of skin so they don't dry hard. "It's just like playing cat's cradle," he says as he ties string to one stem, and then another, and they balance each other draped on the wooden rack. "Then it's ready for two or three or four days outside."

He hands me one to peel, and I do, gingerly but absorbed. The scraping sound of the peeler against the hard persimmon flesh is satisfying. Persimmons are an alternate-bearing fruit: a large harvest one year means a light harvest the following. In Japan there are precise rules for producing high-quality persimmon fruit: rules for growing, pruning, thinning, fertilizing, bark scraping, and harvesting. Tosh prunes, thins, and trains his trees as best he can, but says there are so many other factors—pollination, when the blossoms come out, whether it is raining, whether there is late frost to burn the blossoms—that it's pointless to try to control the trees too much. "I think for the most part if we do have a very large crop, we pretty much assume the following year it's not going to be . . ." His voice trails off and he hesitates as we stand under the shade of a large tree and Mocha tries to tip over the bucket of peels at our feet.

"Well, we call it faith-based agriculture," he says finally. "It seems like the more you think you're getting a handle on things, something comes up. You're not really in control. We quit spraying, we don't spray any chemicals, so we should be overrun with all kinds of damage. And it's really no worse than a mediocre year. It's not perfect, but it's not devastating. So then we look around and we say, okay, well, something's got to be eating these bugs. We've got more birds now, we've got more beneficial insects now, we have more rodents now. And even hawks, and vultures, and rats, and gophers, and coyotes—it just feels more alive. You hear bugs and crickets out there . . . and so it's kind of like, okay, I think we're better off. We can call it nature or creation or whatever, but I think we're better off not tampering with it any more than we need to. And then maybe our definition of what's necessary . . . maybe our definition of 'perfectly clean fruit' changes."

We kneel down in a covered drying room where the persimmons go in their second stage of drying. Aside from the swish of the fan, there is silence as we massage, working our fingers carefully to the fruit's core. The more wrinkles there are, the easier it is to massage. We use our thumbs to push on the ridges at the top and work them into smoothness. We work from the bottom up, work against gravity to bring the liquid back to the stem and distribute it evenly. If we didn't move the liquid on the inside, the creases would stay in the same place for a few days and develop mold.

"Any time we spot mold we take a clean toothbrush, dip it in vodka, and rub the fruit with it ever so gently, and it kills the mold," he says. The goal is to find the right balance, bring it to the point where it is moist but just dry enough, where it has just enough sugar.

I continue to roll them in my fingers, still wet inside the dry skin. As I massage, the glaze breaks and reflects the light. "These are the biggest ones I've seen this year," he says. "I actually picked them up from a retired farmer on the hill." Farmers make deliveries of their fruit during the course of the day, signaled by the chortling sound of truck engines in the driveway, and Tosh buys it from them even though much of it just goes to the food bank. But he figures if he can help them stay in business he will. His biggest obstacle has been water: the cost of water is high in his area and because of bureaucracy and red tape, he pays the regular price, not the agricultural price. But it seems like he may have a bigger obstacle soon. "It seems like very possibly our biggest problem in the near future is going to be the health department," he says, carefully working the persimmon in his hand. "Somebody called us up and said the health department was concerned that we were handling these things and they wanted to be sure that we had hot and cold running water. They haven't come out to visit, but they've been asking about different farms. All they have to say is cease and desist. My guess is we'll end up rebuilding some of these facilities and we'll use glass windows to get sunlight on them. But we probably won't do it outdoors eventually . . . you never know. But I say to people, there's always a good time to quit, too. Hopefully enough people have been trained that they're willing to carry on a tradition, not commercially but personally. And we could conduct classes."

We walk down a dirt alleyway and enter another shed where the persimmons, in their third stage, are placed in paper bags and shaken every day until they are ready for sale. He hands me one and it is like bubble gum in my mouth—bubble gum that then melts and gives way to the essence of persimmon.

He says that the biggest complaint you will hear about dried persimmons is that they are too hard. "What's happening to us as we get more and more refined, we'd like it to stay uniform—that way we know it's going to stay relatively the same. There are some shortcuts, so for some folks I guess they can afford to take them and sell it for less."

The flavor of each piece is different depending on how soft it is, how large it was when it was first peeled, how often it was massaged, whether it was squeezed gently so the moisture came to the surface slowly. As a result, each dried persimmon is a unique moment in flavor and texture, an experience that no one else has had before you and no one will have after you. "So much just depends on eating your own product so you know what it's like, what the variations are, and what the possibilities are for the variations," he says, examining them.

Through another door along the dirt alleyway is the farm stand, where Chris is trying to decide the best way to pack a box of fresh persimmons for mail order. A plump Japanese boy arrives on his bicycle looking for strawberries, and she directs him to the farm stand down the road. She slices open a vodka-treated persimmon and offers it to a few tourists perusing the baskets of fruit. To make these, she adds eight to ten drops of vodka near the stem of each persimmon, puts them in a plastic bag, and leaves them for a week in warm conditions. "As they get riper, they'll get sweeter, really smooth and soft," she says endearingly to the tourists, who are tickled by the novelty. This is a tradition practiced in Japan for centuries, though they didn't necessarily use vodka, but whatever alcohol was on hand. Since it is so difficult to determine whether the chocolate persimmons were indeed pollinated and naturally sweet, this was one way they could ensure that they were sweet. "My mother can spot the pollinated, naturally sweet ones. She's looking at the shape and the color. And she tells me over and over again how to do it, but I'm not good at it." Chris giggles. "A lot of these things are traditions passed down from generations. My parents and grandparents did it, and we're doing it now." Tosh comes from around the corner and teases the customers, "Someone told me his dad would take a big swig of vodka and blow on the stem."

The perfume of baked goods crosses the room as Chris passes out recipes for persimmon cookies, persimmon bread, and persimmon bars to the visitors. Mrs. Otow, who developed the recipes, walks in with her sunglasses on, serious and still silent, and inspects the contents of several boxes. Chris tells me that her mother has a hard time with all of the change. Mrs. Otow was born on this farm with her two sisters, and it has been in the family since 1910. In those days Japanese immigrants could not become citizens, and if you were ineligible for citizenship you couldn't own land in California. "So when they first got here," Tosh says, "they were renting or they were working for somebody. All we know is that they were here working on this piece of land since about 1910."

Even though things are quite different than they used to be for Mrs. Otow, her one constant is massaging the persimmons. That has stayed exactly the same. Tosh stands next to her trying to stabilize the wooden racks as they sway in the wind. "They are dancin' pretty good," he grins. "If someone told me I was going to be sixty years old doing this I'd say they were crazy!" In his effort to keep a tradition going in his retirement, he seems to be busier than ever. When he first started, they were producing four thousand pounds of fresh persimmons, which translated to eight hundred pounds of dried persimmons. Now, he finds himself producing eight thousand pounds of fresh, which translates to sixteen hundred pounds of dried. "We really don't want more business. We want to cut back. We're retired. We're supposed to be taking it easy." He laughs.

We walk down the dirt driveway toward the gurgle of his truck's engine, on his way to buy a couple of truck batteries and deliver boxes of fruit to the post office. "I always wanted to be a dairy farmer," he admits. "But then I said, oh, well, all I really wanted to do was drive a tractor anyway."

He laughs again and takes off down the road, a cloud of dust in his wake, and I watch as the tunnel of persimmon trees engulf him, a thousand tiny suns, glowing and dancing in the breeze.

✒ DRIED FRUIT PUDDING

Adapted from my grandmother Frances Pellegrini.

In my grandmother's home in the Hudson Valley, I found a small black book with my great-great-grandmother's handwriting in it. It is her recipe book, the kind that you don't see any more, novel for how simple the recipes are, with names like "Brown Bread." These are the kind of recipes I wish there were more of, lost in today's modern "haute cuisine." So now when I see them in my grandmother's kitchen or at Mrs. Otow's farm stand, I take note. My grandmother always uses the word "nourishing" as a measure of a food's success. When I make the kind of recipes in my great-great-grandmother's little black recipe book, I understand what nourishing food really is.

There are two versions of this glorious pudding, one simply stewed and blended, and the other baked. What makes it especially glorious is that the first pudding is halfway to the second, so you can decide along the way how far you want to take it. My grandmother enjoys using soy products, so this recipe calls for tofu and soy milk, which makes the pudding lighter and gives it a milder flavor than yogurt and regular milk—though feel free to substitute the latter.

For stewed pudding:

7 or 8 dried unsulphured persimmons, apricots, or mangoes
3 pieces dried papaya about 4 inches long
1 teaspoon ground cinnamon
Pinch of salt
1 cup silken tofu or plain yogurt
1 teaspoon fresh lemon juice

For baked pudding, add:

3 large eggs
¾ cup soy milk or regular milk
½ cup pecans

1. To make stewed pudding: Put the dried fruit, cinnamon, salt, and 2 cups water in a medium saucepan and cook at a low simmer for about 30 minutes, until the fruit is reconstituted and tender. Let cool slightly, then put the fruit and liquid in a food processor and add the tofu. Pulse until smooth, adding the lemon juice along the way, and there you have a quick warm pudding. This pudding is particularly good chilled or slightly frozen, which turns it into a creamy sorbet.

2. To make baked pudding: Preheat the oven to 325°F.

3. Add the eggs and milk to the mixture in the food processor and blend. Add the pecans and pulse 10 times. Pour the mixture into an oven-safe glass bowl and place the bowl in a larger bowl of hot water. Bake for 1 hour until the surface no longer jiggles. Scoop out portions to serve.

MAKES 4 SERVINGS

✳ PERSIMMON DROP COOKIES
Adapted from Helen Otow.

These cookies are more of a cake in cookie form, little drops of pillowy sweetness that taste like fall.

> 1 cup soft persimmon pulp
> ½ cup (1 stick) butter or lard, softened
> ¼ cup honey, plus more for drizzling
> 1 large egg, beaten
> 1 tablespoon baking powder
> 2 cups all-purpose flour
> 1 teaspoon ground cinnamon
> ½ teaspoon ground cloves
> ½ teaspoon freshly grated nutmeg
> ½ teaspoon salt
> ½ cup chopped walnuts
> ½ cup dried currants or raisins

1. Preheat the oven to 375°F. Grease a baking sheet.
2. Blend the persimmon pulp in a blender or food processor and set aside. Beat the butter with an electric mixer until smooth. Add the honey and the egg, continuing to mix, then stir in the baking powder, flour, spices, salt, walnuts, and currants.
3. Drop small round spoonfuls on the baking sheet, 1 inch apart (they will stay relatively the same shape and look like "drops").
4. Bake for 12 to 15 minutes, until puffy but still soft to the touch. They will harden more as they cool. As they are cooling, drizzle the tops with honey to give them a glossy glow.

MAKES ABOUT 2 DOZEN DROPS

✔ FRUIT LEATHER

This is a homemade and healthier version of fruit roll-ups, a childhood favorite of mine. It is also a great way to use overly ripe fruit, especially the kind that doesn't preserve well in other forms. The natural sugars in the fruit will become concentrated as it dries.

2 cups persimmon pulp, or other fruit
1 tablespoon lemon juice
¼ cup sugar (optional, depending on the sweetness of your fruit)
Cornstarch, for dusting

1. Preheat the oven to 150 to 170°F. Puree the persimmon pulp and lemon juice in a food processor. If you choose another fruit, you can chop it and stew it with the lemon juice (and optional sugar) until it softens before pureeing it. Stewing the fruit helps it retain its color. If it is a fruit with seeds, a food mill will remove the seeds more easily than a food processor and strainer. Add a small amount of water to the mixture if necessary so that the consistency is easy to pour.
2. Cover a baking sheet with plastic or a silicon baking pad. The temperature of the oven is low enough not to affect the plastic.
3. Spray or brush with vegetable oil, then spread the fruit puree onto the sheet tray with an offset spatula or knife to ⅛ to ¼ inch thickness. Place it in the oven for 6 to 8 hours. Make sure there is air circulating to prevent scorching. Alternatively, place it in the sun for 6 to 8 hours.
4. Invert the fruit leather onto another baking sheet covered in plastic or a silicon baking pad and oil, and remove the first lining. Place in the oven or sun for another 6 to 8 hours. If it becomes too brittle at any point, simply brush on water with a pastry brush to rehydrate it.
5. Cool the sheet tray and cut the fruit leather into desired sizes. Dust with cornstarch to prevent sticking, cover in plastic, and store in a cool place in a sealed container.

MAKES ABOUT 15 RECTANGULAR FRUIT LEATHERS

JAKE NORRIS

The Whiskey Craftsman

CHAPTER FIFTEEN

Denver, Colorado

Close Your Eyes
and See the Whiskey

J ess Graber is an old rodeo cowboy, a tough old dude. He lives in Woody Creek, up in the woods near Aspen, Colorado, but it is so different from Aspen it might as well be another country. Graber is a volunteer firefighter and a construction worker, and one day, years ago, he responded to his neighbor George Stranahan's barn fire. As the barn burned red and hot in the smoky light, it all came together for Jess Graber—a perfect harmonic convergence.

In George Stranahan's barn that day in 1998 there were rooms once used for butchering cattle that were ideal for conducting practical experiments. Like Jess, George had a passion for spirits, and once he restored the barn, he gave Jess space inside to explore his passion. "I'm an old moonshiner," Jess says, in the slow, low cadence of a cowboy. "I used to make whiskey in 1972 in Netherlands, Colorado. The Christmas list got so big that I started to think, well, hey . . ." Jess began to read and experiment, and before long, George was supplying Jess with mash from his own brewery. As a thank you, Jess named his personal brand of whiskey "Stranahan's."

At about the same time, in Denver, Jake Norris was graduating from college and having an existential crisis. He broke out a note pad and wrote a list of dream jobs: astronaut, superhero . . . but the first thing on the list was whiskey distiller. He was a long way from the subsistence-farming commune he had been born onto, where, before he went to school he'd had to feed chickens and pigs, and collect eggs; where he had designed his first whiskey still at fifteen and became an expert in home brewing. But he decided to forget that first item on his list because he wasn't going to go back to get a degree in organic chemistry; whiskey would just have to be a hobby. He had gone to school for music production, so that is what he did, but he burned out quickly. He soon found himself bartending, still honing his whiskey expertise, still producing small batches and perfecting his craft on the side. Then he met Jess Graber.

Jess met Jake through a friend. "Jake was a self-proclaimed whiskey nerd," Jess says. "My friend said, 'You should go talk to this guy—that's all he ever talks about.'" So Jess went looking for Jake and appeared at the Celtic Tavern in Denver. And it wasn't long before he made Jake his head distiller—the person responsible for getting the grain into the bottle.

"It was like getting called up from the minors," Jake says, zealously. "This is the equivalent of the Black Keys calling me up and saying, 'Hey, would you sing for us? We could really use someone on the road.' This is like being a rock star or a pro football player." Overnight, Jake Norris went from being an avid hobbyist to the head distiller for Jess Graber's whiskey venture, and, together, they laid down their first barrel in January 2004.

I stand in the parking lot of an abandoned factory in Denver where once upon a time a husband and wife made beef jerky. The kitchen in their house became a tad small, so they expanded—and kept expanding until their kitchen took up a city block. There is no sign of life here other than the sound of the empty western frontier in my head. Five feet above ground level is an open garage door that looks into a cavernous warehouse, but there are no steps by which to enter it. Then Jake

Norris appears from the shadows, stocky with a buzz cut that matches the golden stubble on his face. He is holding a metal ladder in his hand that he drops over the side of the building. That is how I enter Stranahan's whiskey for the first time.

"Sloan, baby, what's up?" he says over the phone from his makeshift desk in a shadowed corner to the mechanical engineer. None of the lights work in this new building they just bought to expand their very small whiskey operation. Jess and Jake are bringing whiskey back to the high craft level it once enjoyed. "If you can make something better in your garage than you can get in a store, then it's time for you to go into business." Jake smiles. "I cringe when people refer to whiskey as product. It's not product, it's whiskey. I made it with these two hands. This is about putting fingerprints back on whiskey."

This newest of whiskey companies is unusually conscious of the craft and tradition of whiskey making. "Whiskey was essential to man," Jake says, purposefully promenading on the concrete floors. "When you went out west you had a gun, you had a bedroll, you had a horse, and you had whiskey. It's like a hammer; it's a tool that you must have. It's immortal. It's important to have a connection with where your food comes from, to have a relationship with your food. A lot of people don't get it. In this world, you can get strawberries three hundred sixty-five days a year, and whiskey is one of those things that was always coming from somewhere else. I go out of my way to make sure I'm buying local peaches from Colorado, because it's a car drive away not a three-day trip from China. For me this is an extension of the same thing. It's the opportunity to just zero compromise."

Whiskey is a refinement process in which grains are stripped of impurities and distilled, but, even more, it is a process that represents the history of the people who make it. "The story of whiskey is about people associating it with tradition," Jake says. "We wanted to be our own appellation. We are a Rocky Mountain whiskey."

At the entrance, Kurt, the brewer, is scrubbing down a metal cart. The place is slowly coming together: the distillers, silos, gaskets, and hoses are gradually being installed in their proper places. Stainless-steel silos in the parking lot mark the start of the process. Jake begins to explain it all with a rabid kind of knowledge.

To create alcohol, you need sugar. Whereas fructose is the natural sugar from fruit, maltose is the natural sugar from barley grain. Jake says that thinking of barley like an egg is the easiest way to visualize the process. The husk is the shell, the starchy white material is the white, and the endosperm is the yolk. When a piece of grain germinates, the yolk (endosperm) releases enzymes into the white (starchy white material) and converts those starches into simple sugars. (A starch is just a long chain of sugars, which when cut are simple sugars.) Barley will feed on the simple sugars until it can put down roots and start taking nutrients from the earth. So the malting process is naturally occurring. If someone left out a bucket of grain and it started to rain and sprout, it would taste sweet after a few days.

Yeast can eat simple sugar very readily. It is a natural mechanism for decomposition that, when added to sugar, produces alcohol. There are many different kinds of yeasts (trillions) that all have different purposes. One family of yeast is used to make drinking alcohol; other kinds are used to break down cellulose or produce other chemicals like traced pathogens.

Whiskey evolved from a thirteenth-century beer that was produced using open-air fermentation—in what was essentially a big bathtub. All one had to do was wet the grain and wait for wild yeast to cultivate it, then pour off the liquid and drink it—this was beer. Hops was added later as a preservative and antimicrobial. Now we add hops for flavor. So whiskey evolved from a prehopped thirteenth-century beer—simply malted barley boiled with wild yeast in it.

The problem with open-air fermentation is that uninvited wild yeast and bacteria can settle into the bathtub. In a nutrient-rich liquid filled with sugars and yeasts of varying sorts, the waste of some of the yeast will not be delicious drinking alcohol; it will also be traced with pathogens. And as you distill that liquid down to a more potent state, the alcohol, flavor, and pathogens become more potent as well.

And herein lies the glory of Stranahan's whiskey. The step that Jess and Jake take, that no one else has, is sanitary food-grade fermentation. They sterilize the inside of their brewing vessels, so that when they transfer the liquid into the fermenting tanks, they can introduce one isolated strain of good yeast that has no competition, and where there is no chance of pathogens forming from ambient roaming yeasts. The process of sanitizing the tanks drastically improves the flavor. By keeping the tanks very clean, they are basically preventing bad bacteria from getting in and producing off, sulfur-based flavors with bad chemical components that are harder for the body to process. "If you went out and just drank Jim Beam all night you would wake up in the morning feeling like shit," says Jake. "If you just drink Stranahan's and water all night, you will wake up in the morning feeling remarkably good because it's so clean. And really, that's our big breakthrough."

This also means you can taste whiskey for the love of it, and never have that yelled-too-loud feeling in the back of your throat while drinking it. "It's not that we're crazy geniuses to think of this. The same tradition that all of these whiskey houses are steeped in, they're also mired in. They couldn't change if they wanted to. Who is going to change Jim Beam? Bushmills whiskey is older than our country. When you think of whiskey, you think: history, old, tradition. Bushmills started in 1608, Jameson in 1780. Louis Pasteur didn't invent microbiology until the 1850s, so they were around for two hundred years before anyone viewed yeast through a microscope. They knew that if you put this goop into that goop and waited ten days you could get drunk, but they didn't really know what was going on."

With the advent of microbiology, scientists were able to observe yeast and see that different strains were shaped differently. Then they could separate them and grow them in isolation. They could identify the bad yeast that causes headaches from the good yeast that makes alcohol. Jess and Jake are using this knowledge to their advantage while bringing whiskey back to an artisanal level—this is the advent of pure-breeding in whiskey. "Bushmills, Jameson, Macallan, all of these big houses were already set in their recipe. We came along in 2004 and said, 'Well, how would you make whiskey today?' We looked at what's smart, what makes sense."

Jake and Jess have developed the first original American whiskey recipe since Prohibition. They use 100 percent malted barley because they think it produces a smoother, higher-quality alcohol than whiskey made with a mixture of barley and corn. They don't use corn because it is high in oil. "When you distill an oil, it breaks down into its complex constituents," Jake says, "but it doesn't necessarily assemble them on the other side. So if you think about oil like a pickup truck, you can park a pickup truck in your front yard and it's a truck. If you disassemble the whole truck and spread it across the front yard it's junk. Oil in itself is a useful thing—it's oil. But if you disassemble oil chemically, you just end up with junk. You end up with all the parts that made oil, but not oil. And they break down into the bad chemicals you don't want. Because corn is higher in oil, it's going to produce more impurities. Barley is lower in impurities and has a better flavor."

The grain used in Stranahan's whiskey is similar to that in single-malt Scotch, but it is not smoked. The Scottish smoke their malt to stop the endosperm (yolk) from eating the sugars (white). The Scottish microclimate shaped the flavor of their whiskey. After the British navy clear-cut the land to build ships, the Scots went to the peat bogs and discovered that compressed peat mixed with soil burns at a slow rate, leaving a distinct ashtray flavor they came to enjoy. Jess and Jake don't smoke their malt because they aren't trying to emulate Scotland. "It might sound simple, but it's a really hard concept to get through to people. We're not trying to make Bourbon or Scotch, we're trying to make a new, unique American whiskey."

A truck full of grain arrives every ten days from suppliers within Colorado; sourcing within their state is important to them. They use four different barley varieties—90 percent of the recipe is "meat" barley, and the rest is specialty flavor grain.

The barley is ground by a mill to expose surface area, then sent to a kettle where it is sprayed with hot water while turned in a process called "sparging." The water dissolves the natural sugar, causing the flavor and sugar to bleed from the grain—like tea from a teabag. The sugar water is pumped to a kettle, which is sealed and brought to a boil for an hour. This ensures the death of any unwanted microbes or bacteria that survived the journey. The boiling, in effect, pasteurizes the liquid (which is now called wash). "Now, that's bad in milk, that's bad in apple juice, but it's good in wash," Jake says, weaving among the globular metal pots. "From this step forward everything that this wash will come in contact with is cleaner than an operating room—every single hose, clamp, and gasket is sterile."

From there the boiled wash is sealed in a fermenting tank with sixty gallons of liquid yeast, which grows to 120 gallons of live yeast within a day. As wash goes into the tank, it is injected with pure oxygen, which the yeast eats and colonizes. When the yeast is finished there, it begins feeding on the sugar. "Yeast is like people," says Jake shrewdly. "It will reproduce until it runs out of room, eats all of its resources, or chokes on its own waste."

When the yeast has finished eating all of the sugar the wash is left with 8 percent alcohol. "We could use a genetically engineered strain of yeast the way the big companies do and get 18 percent alcohol," Jake says, leaning against an older copper pot, "but you have to think, if a natural yeast only gets 8 percent, and a genetically engineered can get ten more percent, what the heck is it eating, and do you really want to drink that? You tell that to an accountant, and he thinks you're crazy. You tell that to a craftsman who loves what he's doing, and it makes perfect sense."

In five days, after the yeast has consumed the sugar, the distillers "crash" the tank. The tanks are lined with a thermal medium, a hollow space, which keeps the temperature at 74°F. To crash the tank, the temperature is lowered to the 50s and the yeast goes dormant. It falls to the bottom, settles in a cone, and turns to a solid. Enough yeast for the next batch is reserved, and the rest goes into the drain.

The remaining liquid is pumped to three new tanks powered mostly by solar energy, an expensive venture for a small-batch producer. Alcohol and water boil at different temperatures, and at this altitude, one mile above sea level, alcohol only needs to rise to 174°F to become vapor. "So if I can raise it to one hundred fifty degrees using natural energy, then I only have to raise it forty more degrees using gas energy. You know how much energy that saves? It's phenomenal."

As the alcohol boils, it turns to vapor before the water does. It travels up a column, where the condenser cools it and converts it from vapor to liquid. The result of this first distillation is 100 percent proof, which means it is 50 percent alcohol, 50 percent water.

From there it moves to the spirit still, where a process called "cutting heads and tails" occurs. All of the most dangerous compounds in alcohol have the lowest boiling point. As they come up to a boil first, a selector valve catches and discards them. Then the valve cuts off the last liquid to boil, the water, which means the distillers are left with the essence of their labor: 140-proof alcohol. It is virtual rocket fuel then, so they dilute it to 110 proof with Eldorado Springs water from Colorado, one of the biggest and oldest aquifers in the United States. Then they age the alcohol in six-barrel batches. "Five years after I started, I barreled my one thousandth barrel," Jake says. "Jim Beam at peak production can make one thousand barrels in just over three hours. My process redefines 'small batch.'"

By aging it in new American white oak barrels, Jake and Jess add the final finish to their American whiskey flavor—that vanilla, caramel flavor that comes from the tannin in white oak. The barrels are built the same way they have been for centuries, no screws or nails, fitted together entirely with pressure. The inside of the barrel is burned, and as the heat from the fire penetrates, it caramelizes the natural sugars in the wood, which then travel toward the burn surface and carry with them tannins and lignin (also called vanillin). The fire is then extinguished with water and the sugar caramelizes on the wood, along with a layer of activated carbon, which absorbs impurities.

When Jess and Jake put the whiskey into the barrels, its color is as clear as water. The wood's toasted pores are locked open, and the wood draws impurities out of the spirit while the spirit draws flavor and color out of the wood. Sixty to seventy percent of the flavor and color in whiskey comes from the wood; the rest is from the grain and yeast. This means never using a barrel twice. Single barrel use is one of the requirements for being considered a straight whiskey, so all of the used American whiskey barrels go to Ireland and Scotland. That is why a Scotch might age fifteen years—the barrel is like a used tea bag. An American whiskey, on the other hand, draws out everything it needs from the wood in two years. So age is not an indicator of quality. "Age is a statement of age," Jake says. "That was the biggest breakthrough we have made in whiskey. People think it's too good to be two years old."

When Jake is ready to bottle, he does a barrel sampling. He tastes the contents of each barrel and selects ten to twelve to become one batch. Each barrel has a particular characteristic, and its own personality. He plays with the flavors that come from barrels of different ages, and allows each batch to have its own nuance. Though they will all have the Stranahan's characteristics, each batch will have notable differences, and once a batch is completely sold it is gone forever.

Standing atop a stepladder, peering inside a pot, Jake says, "I like that. Because that's a natural variant. No two batches of gumbo taste the same, but it's all really damn good. Each batch should have its own personality. Accountants come through and they say every batch should taste the same because people want to know what they're going to get and that's how you build consumer loyalty. There's an Applebee's in every town in this country, and it's not because the food is good, it's because people want to know what they're going to get. Some Americans don't like to be surprised. They want to walk in and eat the same shitty burger every time so that they know what it is. They want factory food."

He continues: "And then there are the other people. If I'm driving in a weird part of town and there's a little taquería that I've not seen before, I pull over and try it because you never know, and that's when you find those incredible gems. That's the way I approach everything. One of my favorite things to do when I was a civilian was to go and buy private bottling. When Macallan has a whiskey that doesn't fit its cookie-cutter profile, it's sold at auction as a single barrel."

Jake retrieves bottles of his whiskey to demonstrate that no two bottles are the same. Here, everything is done by hand, including the label making, each one handwritten with the distillation date, the distiller's personal signature, and a comment. "A comment is whatever you want—what book you're reading, what music you're listening to, that you're going to go fishing this weekend. And the idea behind that is to remind people that it's made by people."

He opens a bottle and reveals the vanilla and caramel American whiskey nose. At 94 proof, the whiskey is quite strong. We stick our noses to the spirit, part our lips, and bring in air through our mouths to temper the air coming through our noses. I smell it until I can almost taste it, then take a sip. He tells me to sip it like hot coffee, bring air into my mouth, roll it around my palate. We wait and see what it does. On the first sip, I don't taste much as my palate acclimates. But then I begin to taste it on a second sip and maybe another sip after that.

Then Jake adds water. The optimum proof for drinking whiskey is in the 80-something range. The legal minimum for straight whiskey is 80 proof. That is where the big brands are, because they realized that if they added more water they would make more money by volume. The problem with that is that when you add water, a chemical reaction happens. The oxygen in the water oxidizes the flavor molecules, which is akin to lighting a firecracker. The flavor is ignited but then fizzles out. If you are not there to catch the moment, it just disappears, nobody ever sees the fireworks. "By giving it to you at 94 proof, I allow you to light the fuse at home. If I cut down to 80 proof it has already had its moment in the bottle and no one got to see how good it really is."

Jake adds a few more drops of Eldorado Springs bottled water, the same that he uses when making the whiskey. The first sip shocks my palate again. But as I roll it on my tongue and feel the unpleasantness, I close my eyes, focus on my palate, and see the flavor changing. It moves from a burning sensation to apple crisp to green banana. The flavor moves across my palate, and I can feel it shifting, see different flavors blossoming and collapsing and another flavor coming along. This is called a finish. "This whiskey has one of the longest finishes," he says, sitting atop his metal desk. "It just keeps blooming after you've had your last sip. You're still going to taste new flavors. It leaves a buttery mouthfeel."

With a little more water still, the taste changes again, puts space between the molecules so I can taste it more clearly. It turns into lemon zest and white pepper, then blueberries and cream, then porridge. It keeps changing, flipping, like a fish on a deck. "That's what a well-made whiskey should do. It's 94-proof spirit and it doesn't burn in the back of your throat," he says with a satisfied look.

He hands me a bottle of whiskey with a label that says, "reading Camus." He says, "On a Sunday afternoon, turn off the music, don't let anybody talk to you. Sit there and space out on the flavor of whiskey and write down anything that comes to mind. Break it into attack, middle, sustain. If you do this a little bit, it changes the way you drink. If you pick it apart it's like you're rediscovering the flavor that you're used to."

At a young age, Jake has managed to turn his passion into a career. And he still can't believe it. "The amazing thing about whiskey is that you can go and talk to somebody and ask them what whiskey they drink and it's a source of pride because it's what their dad drank. And it's seriously an extraordinary honor to have been at the helm in the distillery. There's literally maybe a few thousand people ever that have had the opportunity to shape a whiskey, to make a new whiskey that actually goes to market. And to have someone say I drink Stranahan's because my dad drinks Stranahan's . . . I'm part of something that's much bigger than I am. It's phenomenal. I'm not trying to be a mall. I'm not Walmart. I'm Tony's Meats. Do one thing and do it well. Be perfect. And no compromise. That's a life well spent."

✼ WHISKEY SALAD

Really great whiskey is too good to cook. But it is a shame to waste the mediocre kind; it is, after all, whiskey, which is inherently a venerable kind of drink. If your whiskey gives you that pinch in your throat, that vitamin C-in-your-jaw feel, then it is probably mediocre to drink but perfect for cooking. In this recipe, the acid and sweet from the onion and tomato, and the tang of the whiskey, balance each other well.

> *1 large ripe and juicy tomato*
> *¼ sweet onion, diced*
> *¾ cup diced feta cheese*
> *2 handfuls parsley leaves*
> *1 ½ tablespoons whiskey*
> *½ teaspoon salt*
> *Black pepper to taste*

1. Combine all of these things, squeezing the juice of the tomatoes onto the salad to give it a little extra "dressing."
2. Let it sit and macerate in the refrigerator for 1 hour. The longer it sits, the less you will taste the whiskey.

MAKES 1 DRUNKEN SALAD

✉ BOURBON PECAN TART

Adapted from Charles Chocolates, Emeryville, California.

One evening not long ago, I went to visit Charles Siegel and his chocolate factory in California. It doesn't have green elves running around and misbehaved children drowning in vats of chocolate. This is a much more classy place, and it doesn't give me nightmares.

Charles taught me how to make a bourbon pecan tart, which we made while I snacked on frozen hot chocolate, homemade s'mores the size of a small house, tiny champagne grapes dipped in dark chocolate, orange twigs, chocolate-covered almonds, and lavender-flavored truffles. Then, while we waited for the tart to cool, we piped little dollops of bourbon-flavored ganache into gold-speckled casings.

He makes a deep-dish version of this tart because he likes a higher ratio of filling to crust, but it works just as well in a regular tart pan. I adapted this recipe to suit my taste: For example, I use molasses, but corn syrup will work as well. This tart tastes like a sweet nutty cocktail, perfect for the cold holiday season.

For the tart dough:
1¼ cups all-purpose flour
1 tablespoon sugar
½ teaspoon salt
½ cup (1 stick) cold butter, cut into small pieces
1 to 2 tablespoons ice water

For the filling:
¼ cup (½ stick) butter, melted
¼ cup sugar
4 large eggs
¼ teaspoon salt
2 teaspoon vanilla extract
1 cup molasses
¼ cup bourbon
2 cups pecan halves, raw or toasted

1. Make the tart dough: Combine the flour, sugar, and salt in a large bowl, then add the butter and work it with your fingers until it looks sandy. Stir in the water and work until the dough comes together. Form it into a thick disk and refrigerate for 30 minutes or so.

2. Roll the dough out using flour, as needed, to prevent sticking, and fit it into a buttered 9½-inch removable-bottom tart pan, leaving dough above the edges so it has room to shrink. Patch up any holes in the dough with water and scraps of dough to prevent the filling from leaking later. Freeze until firm.

3. Preheat the oven to 400°F. Line the pan with aluminum foil and fill with pie weights or dried beans. Bake for 10 minutes, remove the foil and weights, and bake for an additional 10 minutes, or until lightly browned. Let cool.

4. Make the filling: Using an electric mixer, combine the butter, sugar, and eggs, beating until the sugar is dissolved. Add salt, vanilla, molasses, and bourbon and mix until well blended.

5. Fill the cooled tart shell with pecans (if you want to be a perfectionist about it, turn them all face up), then pour the filling evenly over the top, without letting it overflow. Save any extra syrup to top off with later.

6. Place the tart on a baking sheet (this will capture any syrup that leaks) and bake for about 35 minutes, or until the center is firm. If you find that too much syrup leaks out of the tart and into the pan, simply spoon it back in. It will stop leaking as the heat coagulates the liquid. After 10 minutes, add any leftover syrup to the top to compensate for evaporation.

7. Let cool slightly on a wire rack. Brush the top of the tart with any remaining syrup from the bowl to give it a glossy glow. Serve warm with vanilla ice cream.

MAKES 1 ALCOHOLIC PIE

✤ WHISKEY HOT SAUCE

This hot sauce is hot, but can be adjusted to suit your taste buds. For a medium or mild version, substitute jalapeños or bell peppers for part of the serranos and chipotles, or for an even hotter version, use habanero peppers in place of serranos.

> 2 tablespoons vinegar
> ¼ cup serrano peppers, seeds removed and diced
> 2 tablespoons chipotle peppers in adobo sauce, roughly chopped
> ½ cup onion, finely diced
> ½ cup carrot, peeled and finely diced
> ¼ cup whiskey
> Juice of 1 lemon
> ½ cup brown sugar or molasses
> ¼ teaspoon ground cumin
> 1 tablespoon salt

1. In a saucepan, heat the vinegar with 1 cup of water, and add the diced serrano peppers, chipotle peppers, onion, and carrot. Let them simmer on low heat covered for 15 to 20 minutes to soften.
2. Add the remaining ingredients to the saucepan, stir and return to a simmer for 3 to 5 minutes.
3. Puree in a blender or food processor, transfer to a glass jar and let cool. This can be kept in the refrigerator for up to one year.

MAKES ABOUT 1 ½ CUPS WHISKEY HOT SAUCE

FRANCIS HONORÉ

The Fig Collector

CHAPTER SIXTEEN

Graveson, France

Fig Heaven

A retired tailor from my hometown keeps two fig trees in his backyard. He will spend twenty minutes telling you just how he wraps them to keep them fruitful in a climate where they do not belong. Such is his love affair with figs.

My love affair with figs began in Manhattan at a fruit stand on Second Avenue in early August, where every evening as he was closing up shop, a Ukranian man would push them on me with an almost religious fervor. So it was that I became a convert and learned to love them in an inexplicable kind of way, for their muted smoky sweetness. Two years later, I am living three thousand miles away in an old house I have named Le Petit Chateau. It is situated on the grounds of an ominous, larger stone chateau with stables, and a gardener who pedals around on his bike and lets his watermelons get as big as boulders.

I learn what patience means my first week trying to find food. I have given up on trying to smuggle watermelons out of the garden at midnight, and instead borrow a bike from my roommate and ride forty minutes to Sambuc, a town that consists of one small convenience store, a bar, and a restaurant. When I arrive, the store is closed for the daily *reposer*, so I sit at the restaurant next door to have lunch. There they offer me pâté on bread, the best the semi-somnambulant kitchen can muster at three in the afternoon. I wait for two hours, trying to decipher the French language in the local newspaper splayed across the plastic checkered tablecloth in front of me, finally settling in on my French horoscope. I'm told: "Some handicaps, but don't doubt your attention to different oppositions. Take time to reflect on the problems." I don't feel enlightened about my future, but the pâté is surprisingly good.

Later that afternoon, scooting along beside the fields with my bicycle basket chock-full of buttery yogurt and soft cheese, I stop short in a sky-parting moment. Two very large fig trees with very ripe figs stand on either side of the road. Mouth agape, and by now my affair with figs in full obsession, I consider eating them until I am not anymore. It is here, walking away down the pebbled driveway with a skirt full of fat figs, and the juice of a half-eaten one dripping to my elbow, that I commit to my pursuit of the fig.

Soon I enlist Eric—the man who buys ingredients for the restaurant on the estate on which I live—to help me on my quest. Eric wears his dark long hair in a bun and sports Birkenstocks regardless of the weather. He rolls his own cigarettes by hand, filling and sealing them while driving around in his truck, exuding a strong almond aroma as he puffs. He listens to early Michael Jackson and a medley of jazz, and says, "*Ouais, ouais, ouais*" in a heavy, cigarette-tinged voice.

And then one day, driving along with Eric, it happens: I catch a glimpse of heaven. It is called Les Figuieries and is owned by Monsieur Francis Honoré. At the end of an extensive pebbled driveway, I am greeted by two enthusiastic Black Labs and an even more enthusiastic Francis. He is sixty-four, and a diet of figs and Provençal sun has been good to him. His teeth are unusually white, and straight, and reflect from a permanent grin. He speaks with splendid hyperbole, and it is obvious why. This is a gastronomic wonderland dedicated to 150 varieties of figs, but, more so, it is the summary of a man's life.

He marches, I follow, trying to keep up. And as he goes he speaks a lovely fusion of English and French, all the while pulling down figs the size of my fist from around him. He splits them open, revealing their fuchsia flesh, and hands them to me to eat one by one. I have never tasted anything quite so perfect.

Francis Honoré has spent his life traveling the world in search of new varieties of this sublime fruit and has amassed an unmatched collection on this thirty-acre farm in Provence. He strides under a trellis of vines, weaving from tree to tree, passing over figs faster than I can gulp them. He exhibits a strange combination of animated and elusive, animated about anything that has to do with figs, mysterious about everything else. I sample the saccharin Kalamata figs of Greece, where athletes at Olympia were fed diets of figs to increase their running speed and strength (the 50-percent sugar content made it a virtual candy bar). I bite into the Pastiliere fig from Japan, the region where, according to archeological fossil records, the fig tree found its beginnings. I savor the petit Pingo de Mel from Portugal and the fat Fico Santo from Italy. They are black, white, green, and purple, little bulbous jewels pendulous in the wind as if beckoning to me. They possess other elegant names like Dauphine, Noire de Caromb, and Violette de Solliès. They emanate an indefinable smell of "fig-leaf absolute"—a mélange of hot sun on ripe grass, raw coconut, honey, and tobacco.

Monsieur Honoré's love affair with figs began in 1962 when he returned from a stint in North Africa and settled in Graveson. He began traveling with his wife, and then his children, all the while seeking out figs. His quest took him to the Mediterranean (Spain, Italy, Greece, North Africa, Yugoslavia, Balearic Islands) and to Asia (India, Japan), then to Australia and Tasmania, then to South America (Brazil, Chile). "Figs affect all countries and peoples around the inland sea," he says, wide-eyed, "from the cradle of Roman civilization, to Greek and Middle Eastern lands."

As he marches, he takes a special pride in telling me of his fig journeys to America, listing his favorite states with certainty: California, Oregon, Washington, Florida, Alabama, Georgia, Tennessee, Louisiana, North Carolina, and Southern Mississippi—the ones with a climate suitable for figs. He has seen them all on a cross-country Winnebago trip with his wife. "The best fig," he says slowly, theatrically, "is the one you eat right from the tree!"

Francis's life has been one large quest for one of the world's oldest fruits, and here planted all around us are the results. The varieties represent a kind of time travel, back to the earliest books in the Bible; to 2500 B.C. during the reign of King Drukagina, when Sumerian scribes wrote of figs on clay tablets; among the tomb offerings of dynastic kings; and to Cleopatra, who ended her life with an asp and a basket of figs.

We duck into a green-and-white shed with a cedar-shingled roof. The inside is reminiscent of a dollhouse; antique canning jars that date back to 1880 from his grandmother and great-grandmother line the walls. "My ancestors came from Mediterranean lands, the coast of Provence in the Balearic Islands, and these old jars symbolize generations of tradition," he says.

He dips below his wooden counter and presents a tray of jars filled with various iterations of fig preserves: *Compote de Figues en Morceaux* (Fig Compote with Fig Chunks), *Confiture de Figues Blanches* (White Fig Jam), *Chutney aux Figues et aux Épices* (Fig Chutney with Spices)— ancient pots of ancient fruit begin to fill the counter. He bangs on the jars with long twisted silver spoons as if playing the xylophone. The cadence of his French begins to sound like a song as he conducts; the spoons become his batons. He gesticulates wildly, launching into a monologue on the symphonie of flavor in each pot: "The fig syrup can be used with fig confiture on top of a little foie gras on toast." And then he dives his spoon into a jar. "First you taste the orange, and it isn't until later that the fig comes forward and begins the first notes of its solo . . ." He closes his eyes, purses his lips, and brings his fingers to his mouth.

These confiture win awards every year, he says, closing up each magical pot. Every year at the Graveson peasant market his wife, Jacqueline, enters a competition where she "expresses specific dishes cooking around the fig," and "is met with very good reviews."

Eric, my companion fig hunter, with typical Gallic skepticism, still has chickens and vegetables to retrieve, and is not as impressed as I am—which is perhaps why Francis gives me the presents, instructing me to pick my favorite jars off the shelf to take with me. And as we hop into the truck to leave, he flags me down and presents me with a wooden box full of figs.

As the truck bounces back down the pebbled driveway and out through Provence, I cradle them protectively in my lap, eating them like candy. They are the perfect gustatory accompaniment to the terrain. At this time of year, the sunflower fields are in their twilight days. People are very fond of these fields of yellow, they appear everywhere in pictures and postcards. But what they never show you pictures of are the fields of dead sunflowers, which are more amazing in some ways, expressing something mystical and sincere about the millions of large black pupils staring at you as they fade into winter.

Eric stops in Thor, where we take a mandatory long lunch. In French eating establishments, there is no expectation or intention of change. The very nature of some of the dishes served are an invitation to sit for hours and savor tradition. Tellinees, for example, little clams the size of a thumbnail tossed in garlic and parsley, must be sucked and savored slowly over a long period of time. They set the tone and the pace of the meal that follows. We sip rosé in what seems like a distant universe from the one I once knew as a line chef back in New York City, and I wonder how we ever got annoyed if a next course couldn't be fired after ten minutes. Here the waiters also have a different approach to dining. They seem to ignore you at first until you make them notice. And at the end of the meal, they bend over the table, and together you recall what you have eaten as they scribble it down for the record. By then the water and wine glasses have been blended together into one boozy medley, and taking an inventory of the meal seems like a hopeless pursuit.

Warm on rosé and figs, feeling suddenly fluent in French, I take to the pastry counter at the restaurant with Francis's wooden box of figs and convince the pastry chef to roast them. This poor man who, when not stoned, is in an acute state of paranoia that the head chef is going to kill him, agrees to my request and roasts the figs to the edges of crispness.

The dinner service at an end, and this night marking the end of a long and busy season, the head chef has gathered his mop of hair on top of his head and fastened it in a pink scrunchie. From behind the bar he suddenly turns into a disk jockey like a regular New York City clubber. The music reminds me of my first day at the restaurant, when one of the cooks asked me if I liked the '80s R&B group Salt-n-Pepa, "because it was his favorite." Soon two gangly French men are chasing each other around the room over a container of candied cashews. Later, I walk around the gardens in lantern light with a glass of white wine, stepping over escargot, eating my roasted figs.

～～～

In order to see Francis again, I have taught myself how to drive a manual-transmission car. It is a bright red bubble of a vehicle, and aside from the occasional smell of burnt rubber, I am doing well. My favorite drive is through the tree tunnels of St. Rémy at sunset when the cyprus trees become black spikes against the pink night sky. That is the way to Francis. His driveway is almost impossible to find, but by now I have learned that when you get lost in southern France, look for a carousel. In the center of town, there may not be a post office, but there is always a carousel.

The sun is casting a glow on his stucco house and its powder-blue shutters. The gnarled tree in front of his cedar tasting room throws a stark stripe along the road onto stacked lumber that goes for miles. Inside, Francis is doing his silver-spoon routine with two French tourists, and they are delighted. He pulls flyers from his desk for me and them, showing us all of the markets and fairs he is participating in. "Food fairs in Paris five times a year, Strasbourg, Lyon, Tours, et cetera! And very good Michelin-starred restaurants!"

Then he shows me the jujubes tree, filled with the sweet, tart, olive-size, Chinese dates "Only two per day, though," he warns, waiting for my "Why?" "They're an aphrodisiac!" He cracks up laughing.

Small black pots with little germinating fig trees are lined up in rows, sprouting new generations. "Many people are unaware that the fig tree does not flower," he tells me. "The fruit is the flower! And by pinning a live branch in the ground," he continues, "you can start a new tree. Provence has just the right climate—a warm summer and a mild winter. It is why the figs are excellent and succulent."

"I heal with my figs," he says simply. "Love and passion, leaving the tree to grow with harmony, respect for nature, a rational irrigation, and nonaggressive treatment . . ." His voice trails off as he starts to fill up another wooden box. "I love all the figs, with a slight preference for the black fig Caromb," he says, lining them up neatly in rows. "This variety is well adapted to Graveson. It is excellent fresh, as jam, and is sublime when it is dried."

It is my last week in France, and we walk around eating the last figs of the season together off his trees. There is a sense of drama in the harvest. One day they are all there, one day they have all vanished. As we eat the last from the trees, I tell him that my fig trees at Le Petit Chateau are doing well. There was a minor scare after I mistakenly told one of the cooks how delicious the figs were and a few days later the gardeners arrived with ladders and baskets and my heart sank. Luckily, though, there are more ripening. He tells me that the figs in Turkey are giving him stiff competition because the labor costs for hand picking are so low there. Then we stand in silence, in the pink glow of dusk.

The sun is setting on Provence and on my time there, the crooked arms of the trees are darkening against the lavender sky. Francis calls me *mademoiselle*, as he always does, looking out through the feathery overgrown grass, and I wonder if there is a place anywhere else in the world where I could find someone more devoted to a singular craft. There is a heavy stillness in the air, the kind I feel deep in my marrow. Even though Monsieur Francis Honoré and I don't speak the same language, our mutual quest to discover figs and all their celestial attributes have given us a common language. Here, they are all that matters. This is fig heaven.

✿ FIGS AND MARINATED MOZZARELLA

There is really no wrong way to cook and consume a fig. I have even spent many evenings with a flashlight trying to find a few ripe figs from an unready tree, and had to settle on unripe ones—when cooked, they taste lovely, too. Toss them in anything: pasta, salad, a martini . . . everything is better with a fig.

   This recipe is translated and adapted from Francis's French. Like much of the cooking in Provence, it is remarkably simple and lets the pure ingredients speak for themselves.

>   *1 large ball fresh mozzarella cheese*
>   *1 teaspoon walnut oil*
>   *1 teaspoon good olive oil*
>   *Juice of 1 lemon*
>   *1 clove garlic, minced*
>   *Salt and black pepper to taste*
>   *1 tablespoon fresh mint cut into thin ribbons*
>   *8 fresh black figs*

1.   Thinly slice the mozzarella.
2.   In a bowl, mix together the oils, lemon juice, garlic, and salt and pepper. Pour the mixture over the mozzarella and marinate in the refrigerator for at least 2 hours, turning once or twice.
3.   Wash and slice the figs in any way that you please and serve them on a platter, alternating with the mozzarella. Drizzle with marinade, sprinkle with the mint, and season with a few more turns of pepper. Voilà!

MAKES 4 SERVINGS

✳ GAME BIRDS AND FIGS

Figs are a perfect complement to game birds, though the birds are sometimes hard to come by unless you hunt. If they are not at the grocery store, a good butcher can certainly get them for you. Guinea hen, pigeon, pheasant, or even Cornish hen are all suitable substitutes, though cooking times will vary.

> 2 partridges, or 4 quail
> Salt and black pepper
> 2 tablespoons butter, plus more for the birds
> 12 fresh black figs
> 2 tablespoons Port
> ½ cup heavy cream
> 1 tablespoon Cognac

1. Preheat the oven to 450°F.
2. Clean the partridges and pat them dry with paper towels. Season with salt and pepper on all sides, and slip shavings of butter underneath the skin. Put them in a roasting pan and roast for 15 to 20 minutes, until golden brown. Let rest for 10 minutes.
3. Melt the 2 tablespoons butter in a skillet or saucepan over medium heat and add the figs. Drizzle with the Port. Cover and cook over low heat for about 10 minutes, until soft. Season with salt and pepper and at the very end add the cream. Keep warm.
4. Cut the partridges in half and arrange them on a warmed serving platter. Place the roasting pan on the stovetop over low heat, add the Cognac, and stir to scrape up all the browned bits from the bottom of the pan. Cook to reduce the pan juices. Sprinkle the juices over the partridge halves and garnish with the figs and cream.

MAKES 4 SERVINGS

✒ TILAPIA WITH SWEET AND SOUR FIG SAUCE

This fig sauce will go well with other mild white fish, as well as with chicken and pork. The sweet and tangy components immediately brighten any otherwise bland dish.

> 2 onions, diced
> 4 tablespoons olive oil
> Peel of 1 lemon, thinly sliced
> 12 fresh black figs, 4 chopped into small pieces and 8 left whole
> 1 (2-inch) piece fresh ginger, grated
> 1 tablespoon honey
> 4 tilapia fillets, skin on
> Salt and black pepper to taste

1. Preheat the oven to 400°F.
2. In a sauté pan, sweat the onions in 1 tablespoon of the oil over medium heat for about 5 minutes, until translucent, adding 1 teaspoon salt and the lemon peel after 1 minute. Add the chopped figs and the ginger and sauté for 2 minutes, stirring constantly. Stir in the honey and 3 teaspoons water and simmer for 20 minutes, adding salt and pepper, as needed.
3. Place the 8 whole figs in a baking dish and sprinkle them with 1 tablespoon of the oil. Add salt and pepper, to taste, and 1 tablespoon water. Roast for 10 minutes, basting with a bit of water as needed.
4. In a large skillet, heat the remaining 2 tablespoons oil and add the tilapia fillets, skin side down. After 2 minutes, lower the heat slightly, cover, and cook for another 2 minutes.
5. Arrange the fillets on serving plates and distribute the roasted figs around them. Spoon on the fig sauce. Bon appétit!

MAKES 4 SERVINGS

✒ FIG VINEGAR

Fruit vinegars are a great way to enhance the flavor of almost anything. You can use them to deglaze the pan of a roasted chicken or pork chop, add them to green salads and fruit salads, or add them to sparkling water for a tangy beverage. Instead of figs, you can use strawberries, peaches, cherries, or any variety of fruit that's in season, simply keep the ratio of vinegar to fruit at 1:1. You can also play with other seasonings, such as star anise, fennel, caraway, or lemongrass, and see which fruits pair best with the various flavors.

1 pound figs
1 cup white wine vinegar
Fennel seeds, to taste (optional)
Sugar or honey, to taste

1. Remove the stems from the figs and chop them well to expose the inner flesh.
2. Combine with the vinegar and fennel seeds in a glass container with a lid (a mason jar or recycled pickle jar works well), and store for 2 weeks in a cool, dark area. After two weeks taste the mixture to see if it is fruity enough for your tastes. You can add more fresh fruit and repeat the process if you'd like it stronger.
3. Strain the liquid with a fine mesh strainer, into a non-reactive saucepan and add honey or sugar to taste. Bring to a simmer for 2 to 3 minutes uncovered, then turn off the heat and skim off any foam.
4. Strain the liquid into dry sterilized glass jars. (You can easily sterilize them by running them through the dishwasher.) Store the fruit vinegar tightly sealed in a cool dark place.

MAKES ¼ CUP FRUIT VINEGAR

A TO-DO LIST FROM ME TO YOU

Grow baby greens in a window box.

Grow herbs in pots indoors.

Make infused oils and vinegars.

Dry your own herbs.

Bake bread.

Forage for wild edibles.

If you eat meat, hunt.

Keep honeybees.

Start a compost pile in your yard
and a compost bucket in your kitchen.

Keep chickens.

Grow potatoes in pots or even a garbage bag.

Pick wild berries and make jams.

After you eat fruit, try planting the seeds.

Squeeze your own juice.

Can everything so you get to eat it yearround.

Make your own butter from grass-fed milk.

Make your own ice pops.

Pickle vegetables and fish.

Make your own alcohol and spirits.

Make wreathes out of vines.

Make lots of pesto and freeze it.

Or, at the very least . . .

Learn how to make a damn good pie.

THOSE WHO HAVE CAPTURED
MY HEART AND IMAGINATION

David Langford
Lissadell House
Ballinfull, County Sligo
Ireland
00353 71 9163150
langfords@eircom.net
www.lissadellhouse.com

Allan Benton
Benton's Smoky Mountain
    Country Hams
2603 Highway 411
Madisonville, TN 37354
(423) 442-5003
info@bentonshams.com
www.bentonshams.com

Marion Bush
Wild Harvest
marion_bush@yahoo.com

Matthias Trum
Schlenkerla
Dominikanerstrasse 6
96049 Bamberg
Germany
49 (951) 56060
E. service@schlenkerla.de
www.schlenkerla.de

Marc Buzzio
376-378 Eighth Avenue
New York, NY 10001
(212) 736-7376
info@sausage4u.com
www.salumeriabiellese.com

**Jean-Benoît and
    Catherine Hugues**
Mas de l'Olivier
1 3520 Les Baux de Provence
France
33 (0) 490 545 086
info@castelas.com
www.castelas.com

Bill Best
Sustainable Mountain Agriculture
    Center
1033 Pilot Knob Cemetery Road
Berea, KY 40403
(859) 986-3204
bill_best@heirlooms.org
www.heirlooms.org

Hans-Otto Johnsen
Rognenyr
Posboks 1764
Skjeberg
Norway
47 90962799

Jon Rowley
2920 Boston Street
Seattle, WA 98199
(206) 963-5959
rowley@nwlink.com

Karen Weinberg
and Paul Borgard
3-Corner Field Farm
1311 County Route 64
Shushan, New York 12873
(518) 854-9695
dairysheepfarm@aol.com
www.dairysheepfarm.com

Sue Forrester
Cream of Cumbria, Howberry
Blackford
Carlisle, Cumbria CA6 4EN
United Kingdom
44 01228 675558
www.creamofcumbria.co.uk

Steven Wallace
The Omanhene Cocoa Bean
    Company
5441 S. 9th Street
Milwaukee, WI 53221 USA
(414) 744-8780
www.omanhene.com

Rhoda Adams
Rhoda's Famous Hot Tamales
714 Saint Mary Street
Lake Village, AR 71653
(870) 265-3108

Tosh and Chris Kuratomi
6232 Eureka Road
Granite Bay, CA 95746
(916) 791-1656
otoworchard@yahoo.com
www.otoworchard.com

Jess Graber and Jake Norris
Stranahan's Whiskey
200 South Kalamath Street
Denver, CO 80223
(303) 296-7440
www.stranahans.com

Francis Honoré
Les Figuières
Mas de Luquet
13690 Graveson
Provence, France
33 04 90 95 72 03
infos@lesfiguieres.com
www.lesfiguieres.com

Stuart and Anissa Hull
Tellico Grains Bakery
105 Depot Street
Tellico Plains, TN 37385
(423) 253-6911
info1@tellico-grains-bakery.com
www.tellico-grains-bakery.com

Rod Morrison
Rocky Mountain Organic Meats
1201 7th Street
Powell, WY 82435
1-877-754-4606
info@rockymtncuts.com
www.rockymtncuts.com

Chuck Siegel
Charles Chocolates
6529 Hollis Street
Emeryville, CA 94608
(510) 652-4412
info@charleschocolates.com
www.charleschocolates.com

The Ginger Pig
Grange Farm
Levisham
Pickeringm, North Yorkshire
    YO18 7NL
United Kingdom
44 01751 460091
enquiries@thegingerpig.co.uk
www.thegingerpig.co.uk

John Natlacen
Churchmouse Cheeses
4 Market Street
Kirkby Lonsdale, Cumbria
    LA6 2AU
United Kingdom
44 015242 73005
info@churchmousecheeses.com
www.churchmousecheeses.com

Annette Gibbons
Ostle House
Mawbray
Maryport, Cumbria CA15 6QS
United Kingdom
44 01900 881356
annette@cumbriaonaplate.co.uk
www.cumbriaonaplate.co.uk

Martyn Reynolds
Burbush's
Gilwilly Road
Gilwilly Industrial Estate
Penrith, Cumbria CA11 9BL
United Kingdom
44 01768 863841
info@burbushs.co.uk
www.burbushs.co.uk

Neal's Dairy Yard
6 Park Street
London SE1 9AB
United Kingdom
44 020 7367 0799
boroughshop@nealsyarddairy.
   co.uk
www.nealsyarddairy.co.uk

Justin Philips
Beer Table
427 B 7th Avenue
Brooklyn, NY 11215
(718) 965-1196
info@beertable.com
www.beertable.com

Mike Trigiani
Zackie's Original Hot Dog
1201 5th Avenue
North Nashville, TN 37208
(615) 291-8311
www.zackies.com/contact-us
www.zackies.com

Farmer Al
Frog Hollow Farm
P.O. Box 2110
Brentwood, California 94513
(888) 779-4511
www.froghollow.com/contact-us
www.froghollow.com

The Drunken Duck
The Drunken Duck Inn
Barngates
Ambleside, Cumbria LA22 0NG
United Kingdom
44 01539 436347
info@drunkenduckinn.co.uk
www.drunkenduckinn.co.uk

Ristorante Il Latini
Via dei Palchetti, 6
50123 Firenze (Toscana), Italy
39 055 210916
info@illatini.com
www.illatini.com

Caroline and Leonie Fairbairn
Thornby Moor Dairy
Crofton Hall Thursby
Carlisle, Cumbria CA5 6QB
United Kingdom
44 01697 345555

A. Gold
42 Brushfield Street
London E1 6AG
United Kingdom
44 020 7247 2487

METRIC CONVERSION CHART

Weight Equivalents

The metric weights given in this chart are not exact equivalents, but have been rounded up or down slightly to make measuring easier.

AVOIRDUPOIS	METRIC	AVOIRDUPOIS	METRIC	AVOIRDUPOIS	METRIC
¼ oz	7 g	7 oz	200 g	15 oz	425 g
½ oz	15 g	8 oz (½ lb)	225 g	16 oz (1 lb)	450 g
1 oz	30 g	9 oz	250 g	1 ½ lb	750 g
2 oz	60 g	10 oz	300 g	2 lb	900 g
3 oz	90 g	11 oz	325 g	2 ¼ lb	1 kg
4 oz	115 g	12 oz	350 g	3 lb	1.4 kg
5 oz	150 g	13 oz	375 g	4 lb	1.8 kg
6 oz	175 g	14 oz	400 g		

Volume Equivalents

These are not exact equivalents for American cups and spoons, but have been rounded up or down slightly to make measuring easier.

AMERICAN	METRIC	IMPERIAL
¼ t	1.2 ml	
½ t	2.5 ml	
1 t	5.0 ml	
½ T (1.5 t)	7.5 ml	
1 T (3 t)	15 ml	
¼ cup (4 T)	60 ml	2 fl oz
⅓ cup (5 T)	75 ml	2 ½ fl oz
½ cup (8 T)	125 ml	4 fl oz
⅔ cup (10 T)	150 ml	5 fl oz
¾ cup (12 T)	175 ml	6 fl oz
1 cup (16 T)	250 ml	8 fl oz
1 ¼ cups	300 ml	10 fl oz (½ pt)
1 ½ cups	350 ml	12 fl oz
2 cups (1 pint)	500 ml	16 fl oz
2 ½ cups	625 ml	20 fl oz (1 pint)
1 quart	1 liter	32 fl oz

Oven Temperature Equivalents

OVEN MARK	FAHRENHEIT	CELSIUS	GAS
Very cool	250-275	130-140	½-1
Cool	300	150	2
Warm	325	170	3
Moderate	350	180	4
Moderately hot	375	190	5
	400	200	6
Hot	425	220	7
	450	230	8
Very hot	475	250	9

RECIPE INDEX

~ INDEX ~

ACKNOWLEDGMENTS

Thank you to . . .

Brettne Bloom—a ninja agent who put faith in an unknown girl calling her from a phone booth in the south of France.

Dervla Kelly—my editor who ushered me through this process with the utmost sensitivity and good humor; and Luisa Weiss for opening the door to make it possible.

T. Kristian Russell—a particularly gifted visionary who inspires me.

Roger Pellegrini—an exceptional writer and editor who taught me that mastery doesn't create passion, passion creates mastery.

Maureen Pellegrini—who taught me the intimate relationship between food, mind, and body.

Gordon Pellegrini—who teaches me by example that sometimes you just have to roll with things.

Frances Pellegrini—who teaches me how to see life through a different lens.

The Lepori Family—who taught me from birth that love and food are interchangeable.

Those in this book, for their extraordinary generosity in sharing their world with me.

The Libera Boys Choir—my muse.

My friends who have offered words of wisdom, an editorial eye, or a cup of tea along the way: Abigail Cleaves, Emily Goldman, Worth Williams, Faith McCormick, Kelsey Contreras, Mackenzie Chambers, Jamie Levine, Julia Cheringal, Suzy Goldman, Thomas Russell, Mary Ortiz, Jessica Cannon, Christine Carroll, Kamala Nair, Jessica Colley, Sierra Schaller, Alexej Steinhardt, Rona Padua Vergne & David Vergne, Freddie Black, Debbie & Paul Michael, and Nicole Hill Gerulat.

I am very grateful.